PAPER

AIRLPANES

THE HiSTORY OF PAPER AiRPLANES

THE PAPER AiRPLANE iS A FORM OF FOLDiNG PAPER CALLED ORiGAMi AND COMES FROM ANCiENT CHiNA.

MANUFACTURE OF PAPER ON A WIDESPREAD SCALE TOOK PLACE iN CHiNA 500 BCE, AND ORiGAMi AND PAPER FOLDiNG BECAME POPULAR WITHiN A CENTURY OF THiS PERiOD. THE POPULARiTY OF PAPER AiRPLANES REALLY "TOOK OFF" AND iN THE NEXT THOUSAND YEARS iT WAS CHANGED WITH HUNDREDS ON NEW AND EXCiTiNG CREATiONS TO THE POiNT THERE WERE COMPETiTiONS TO SEE WHO COULD MAKE THEiR PLANE FLY LONGEST HiGHEST AND LOOP MORE FLiPS THAN ANY OTHER.

EVENTUALLY THE PAPER AiRPLANE HELPED iN CREATiNG THE FiRST AiRCRAFT DESiGN. ONE OF THE EARLiEST WAS iN 1909. iN 1930 JACK NORTHROP (CO-FOUNDER OF THE LOCKHEED CORPORATiON) USED PAPER PLANES AS TEST MODELS FOR LARGER AiRCRAFT AND iN GERMANY, DURiNG THE GREAT DEPRESSiON, DESiGNERS AT HEiNKEL AND JUNKERS FOUND A WAY OF FLYiNG PAPER MODELS TO ESTABLiSH BASiC PERFORMANCE AND STRUCTURAL FORMS iN TACTiCAL BOMBER PROGRAMS, SUCH AS THE HEiNKEL 111 AND JUNKERS 88.

INSTRUCTIONS

CUTTING OUT THE PAGE

HAVE YOUR PARENTS OR A GROWN-UP HELP CUT OUT THE PAGES YOU ARE GOING TO FOLD TO MAKE YOUR AIRPLANES. THEY CAN USE A BLADE OR SCISSORS TO CAREFULLY CUT ALONG THE EDGE OF THE PAGE AT THE BINDING EDGE TO MAKE A CLEAN CUT.

IF YOU THINK YOUR SKILLS ARE GOOD ENOUGH, GET SOME PRINTER PAPER AND PRACTICE GETTING IT RIGHT.

ITS OK TO MAKE MISTAKES!

FOLD LINES

THE FOLD LINES ARE VERY IMPORTANT AS GUIDES TO YOUR FOLDING PERFECTION, IT'S OK IF THE FOLD IS A BIT OFF BUT THE FLIGHT OF YOUR PLANE MIGHT BE AFFECTED.

NUMBERS

THE NUMBER THAT LOOKS LIKE THIS ❶ IS THE ORDER OF THE FOLDS TO THE INSTRUCTIONS. TRY NOT TO HURRY AND TAKE YOUR TIME AND IT WILL BE THAT MUCH BETTER!

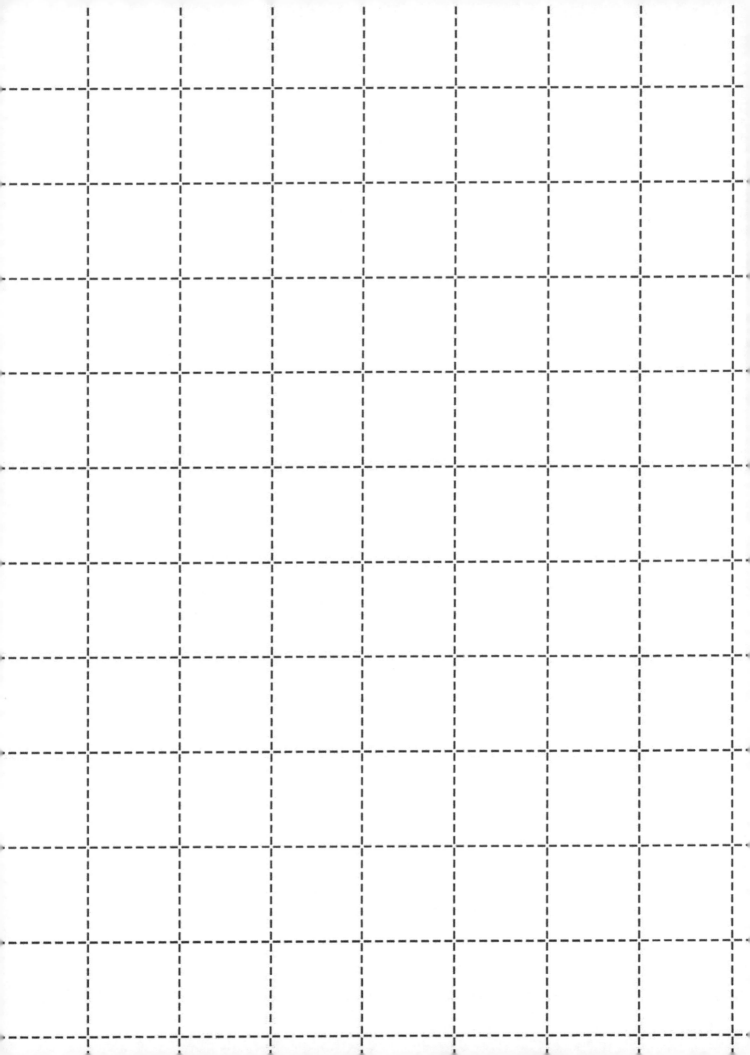

ORIGAMI PLANE - The Basic

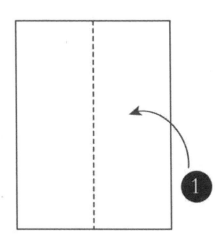

1. Fold the paper in half.

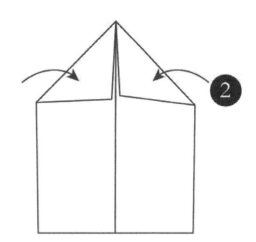

2. Unfold and then fold the top two corners into the center line.

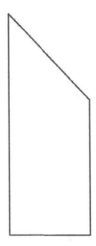

3. Again, fold the paper in half.

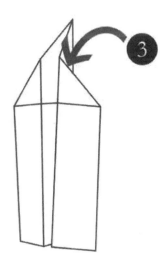

4. Finally, fold the edges down to meet the bottom of the body.

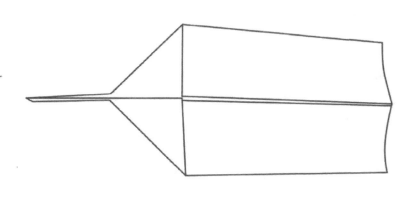

Final Paper Airplane Design
Use a little tape to keep the wings together. If it tends to fly sharply upwards, stall, and then drop straight down, try bending the back of the wings down just a little bit.

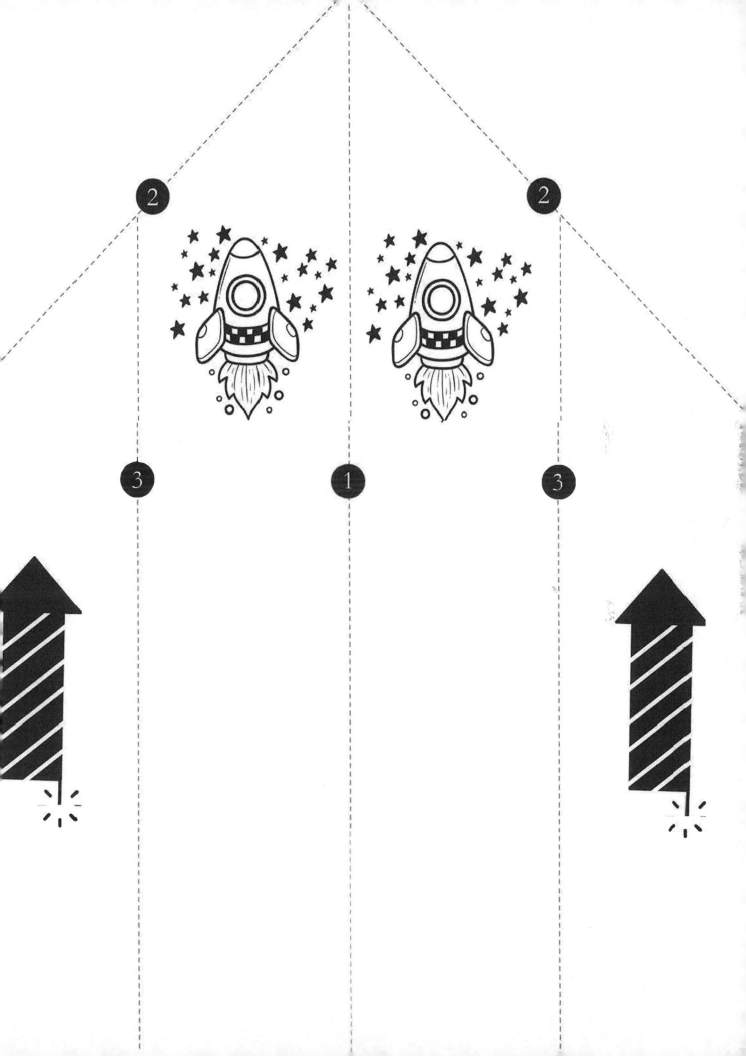

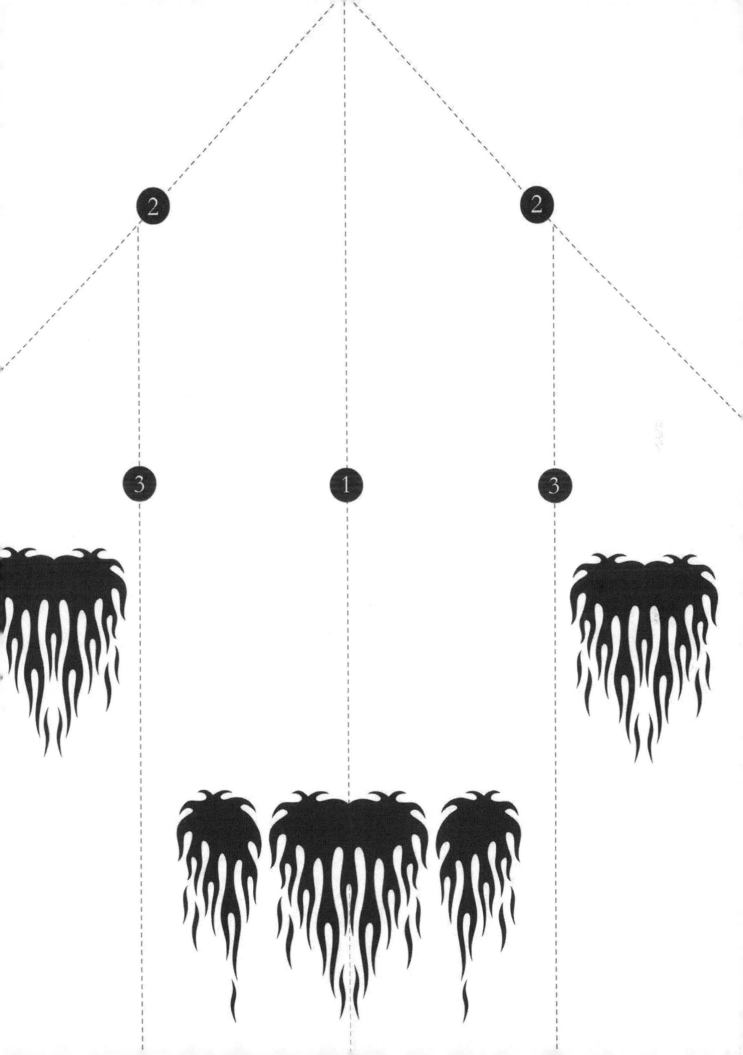

DELIVERY
PREMIUM

DELIVERY
PREMIUM

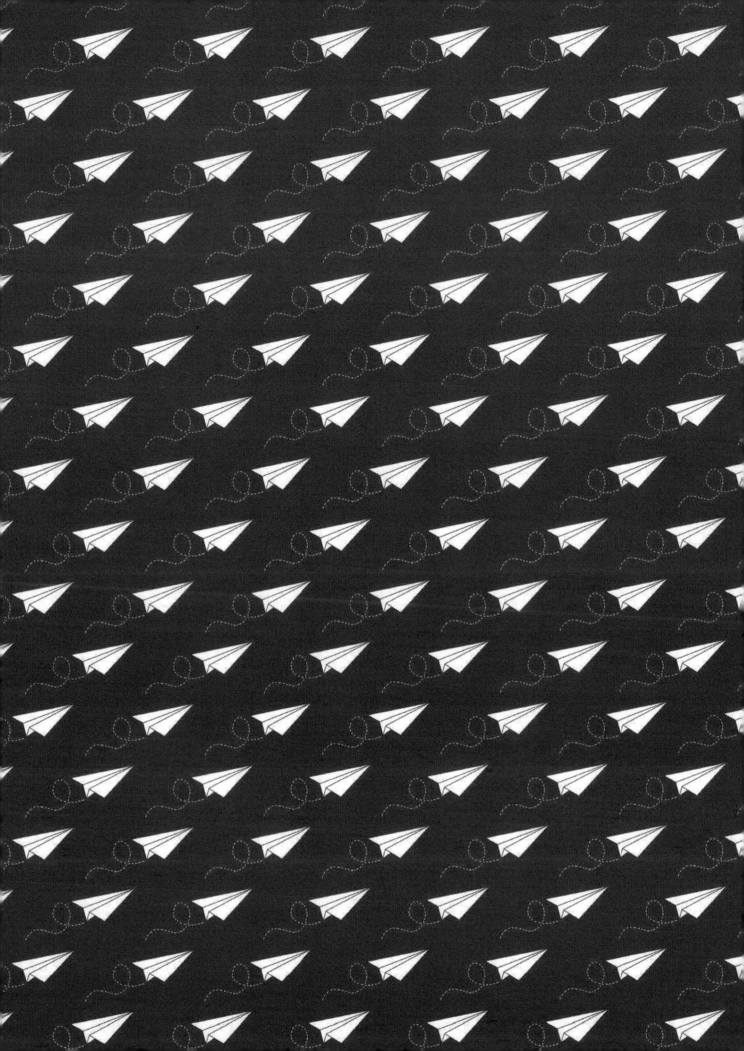

ORIGAMI PLANE - Basic Dart

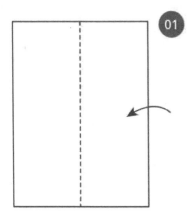

Fold the paper in half.

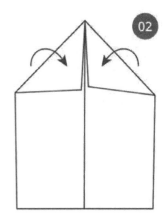

Unfold and then fold the top two corners into the center line.

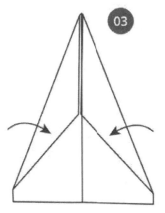

Fold the top edges to the center.

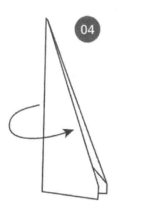

4. Fold the plane in half.

5. Fold the wings down to meet the bottom edge of the planes body.

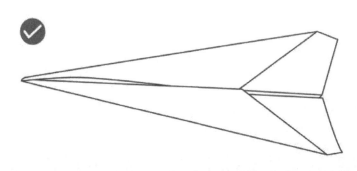

Final Paper Airplane Design

This airplane has stiff wings, so it can tolerate fast throwing speeds. Throw it as hard as you can for maximum distance and speed.

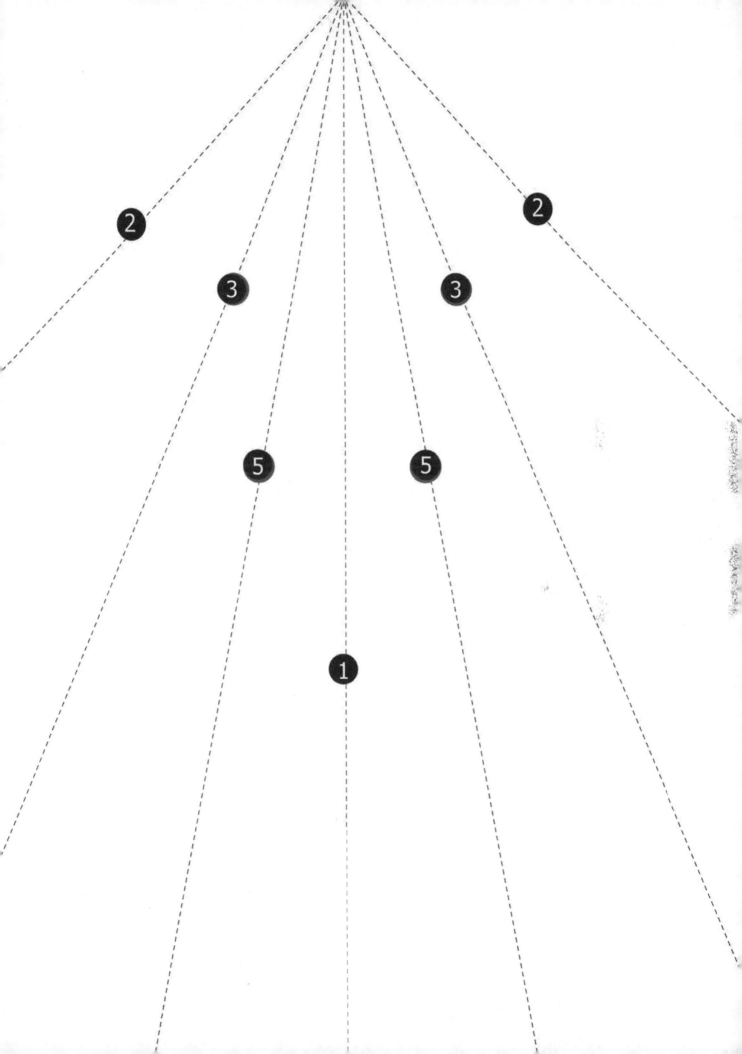

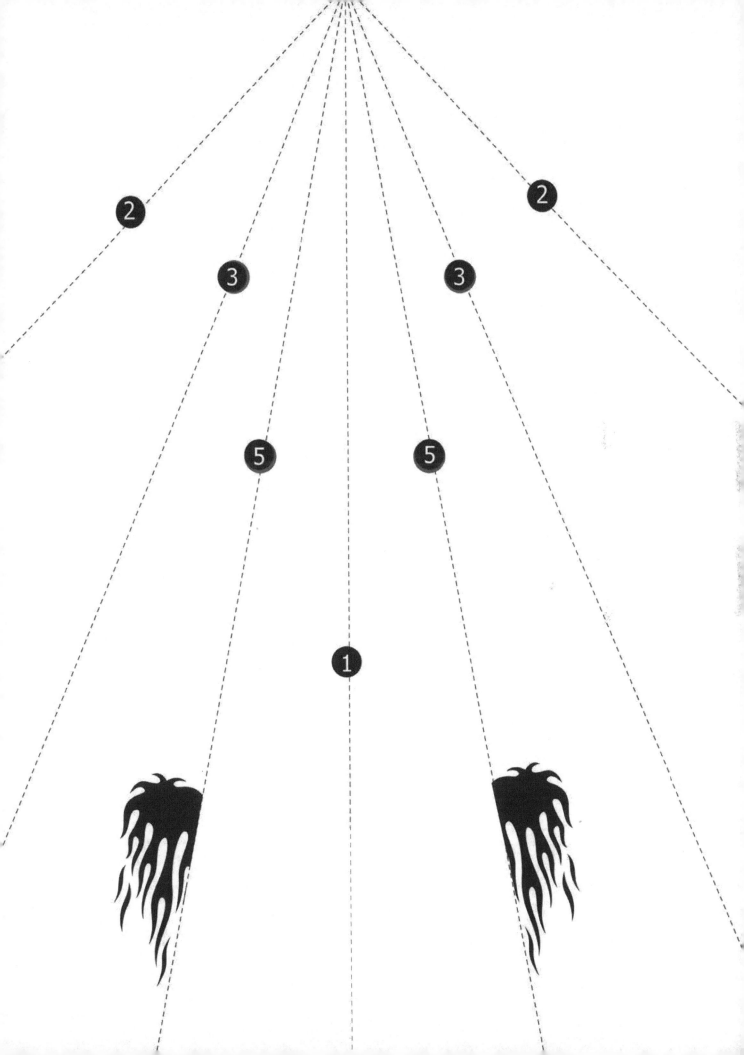

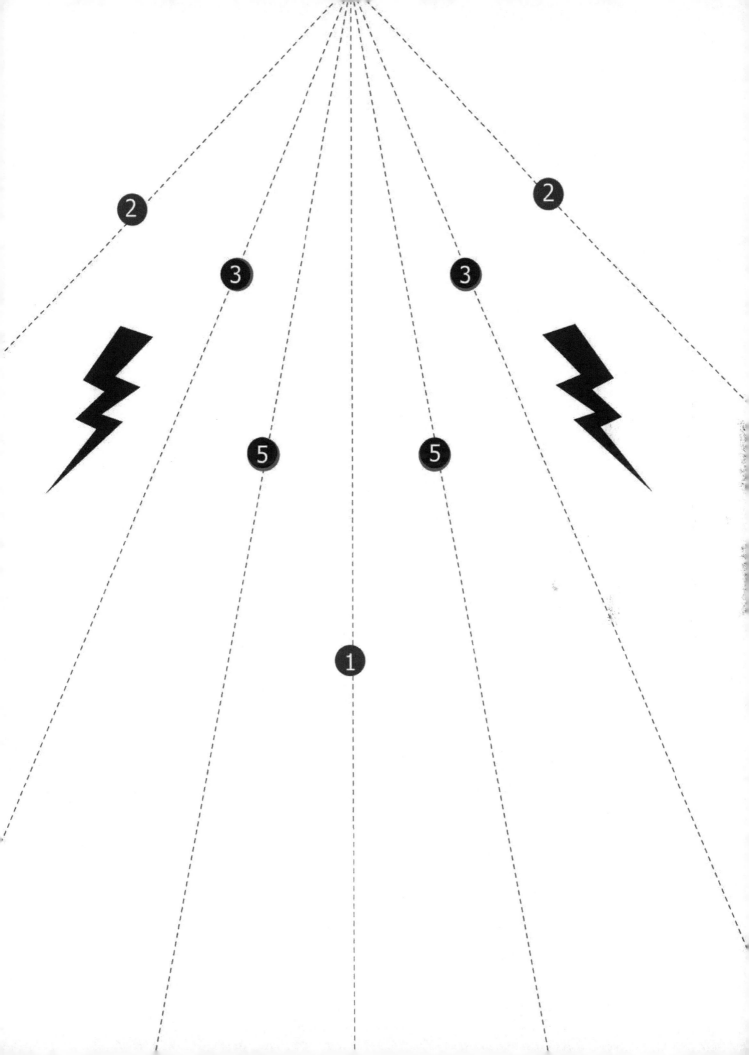

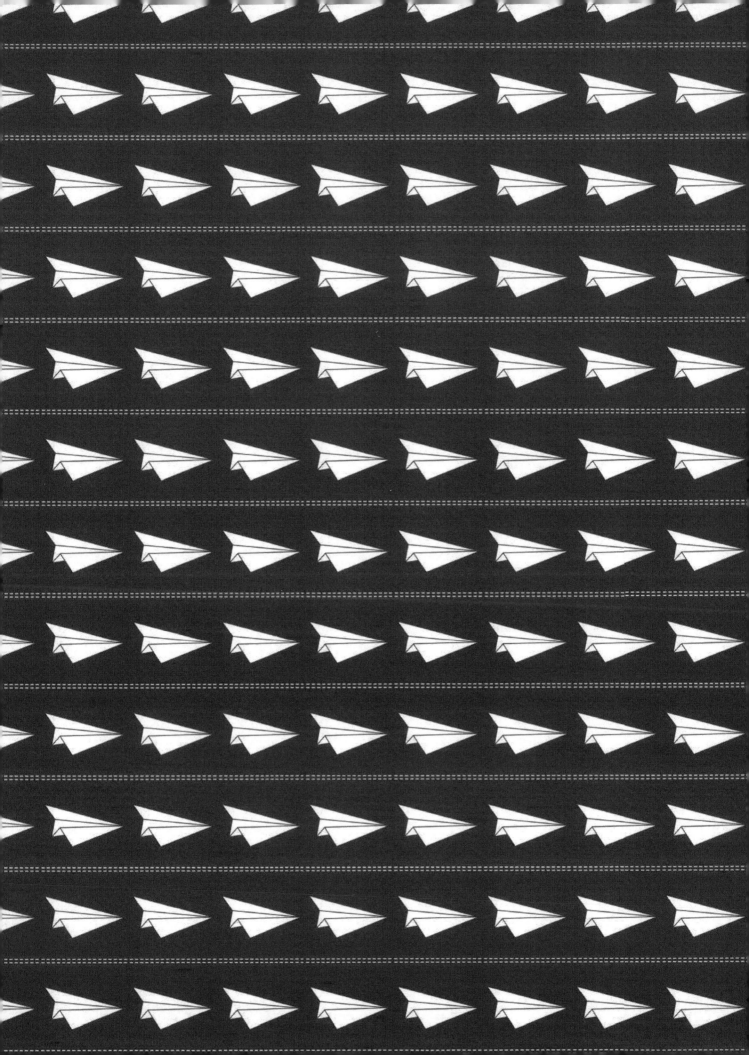

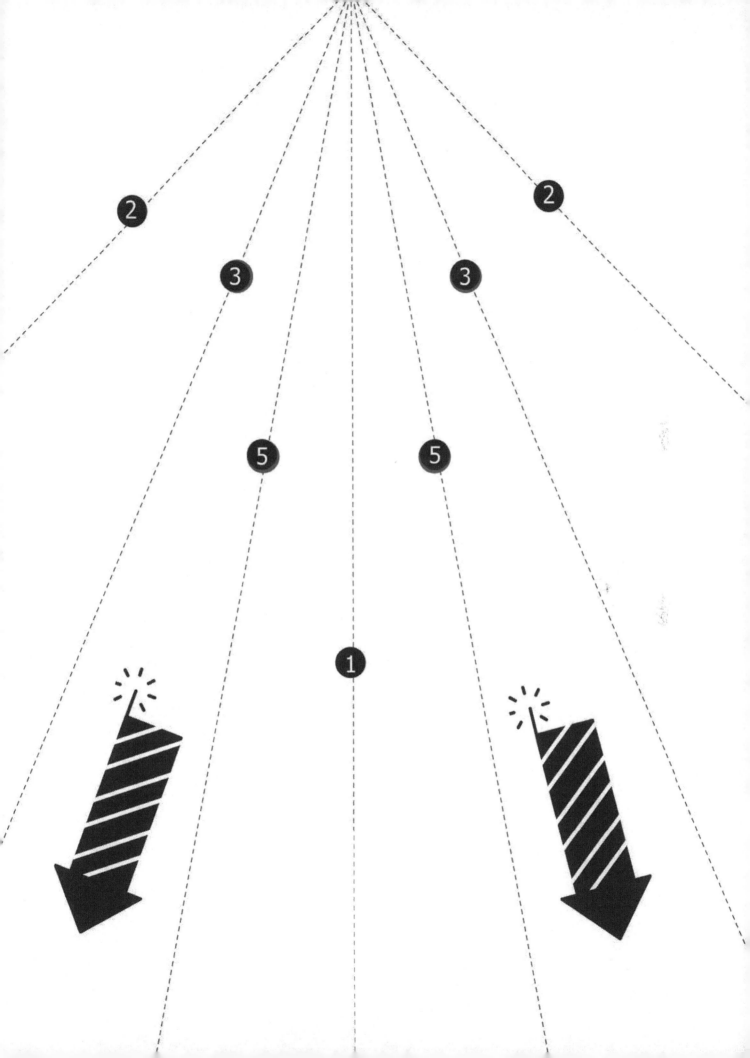

MEDIUM FLYERS

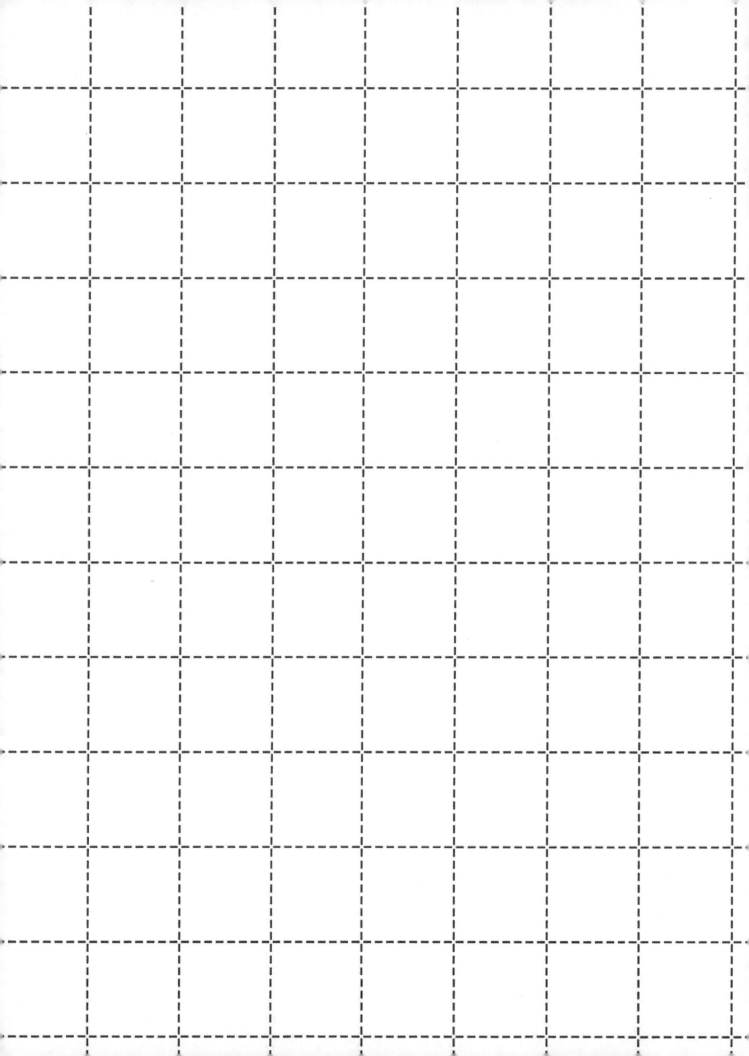

ORIGAMI PLANE - Heavy-Nosed

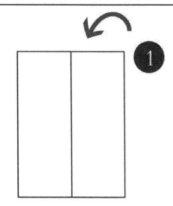

1. Fold the paper in half.

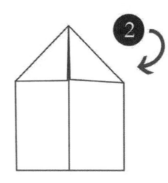

2. Fold the top corners to the center line

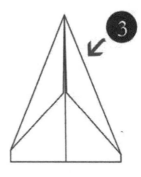

3. Fold the upper sides to the center line.

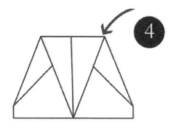

4. Fold the peak to the bottom edge of the paper.

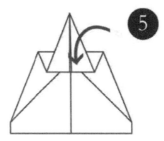

5. Now, fold the peak back up about 2 1/2 inches past the top edge.

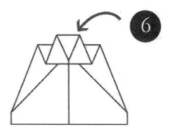

6. Fold the peak back down to the edge of the previous crease.

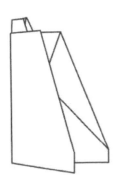

7. Fold the plane in half towards you.

8. Finally, fold both sides down to create the wings.

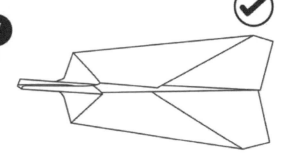

Final Paper Airplane Design
Experiment with the distances that you fold the tip back and forth to adjust how much weight is put into the nose. If you make the nose very heavy, you can make this airplane fly loops.

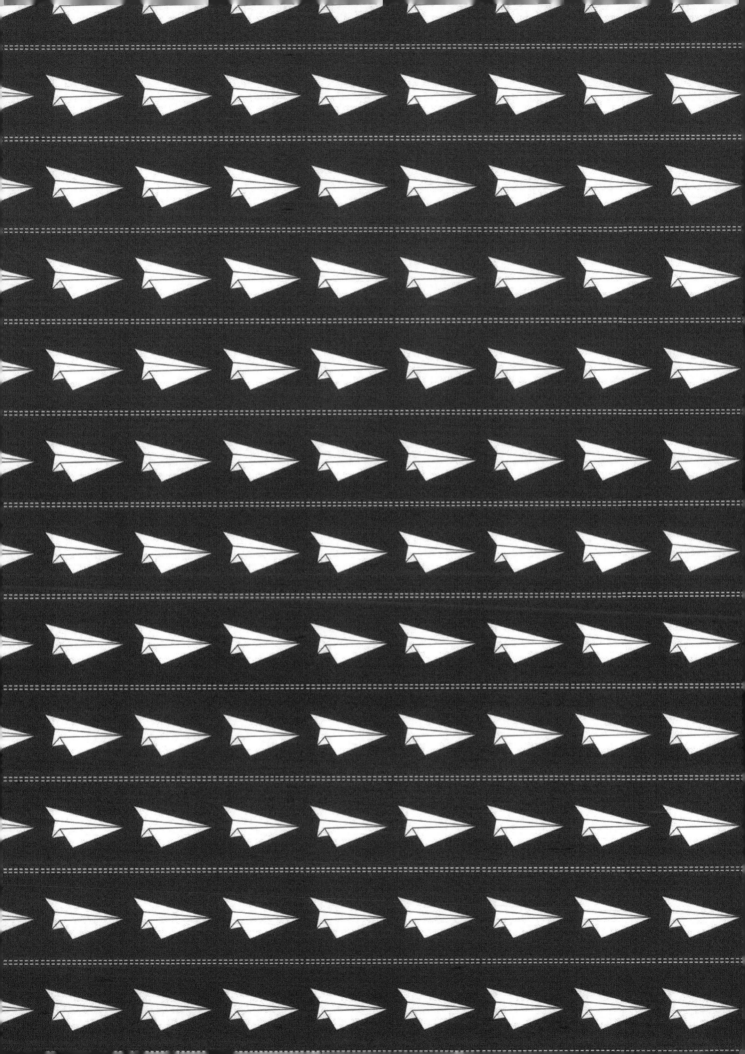

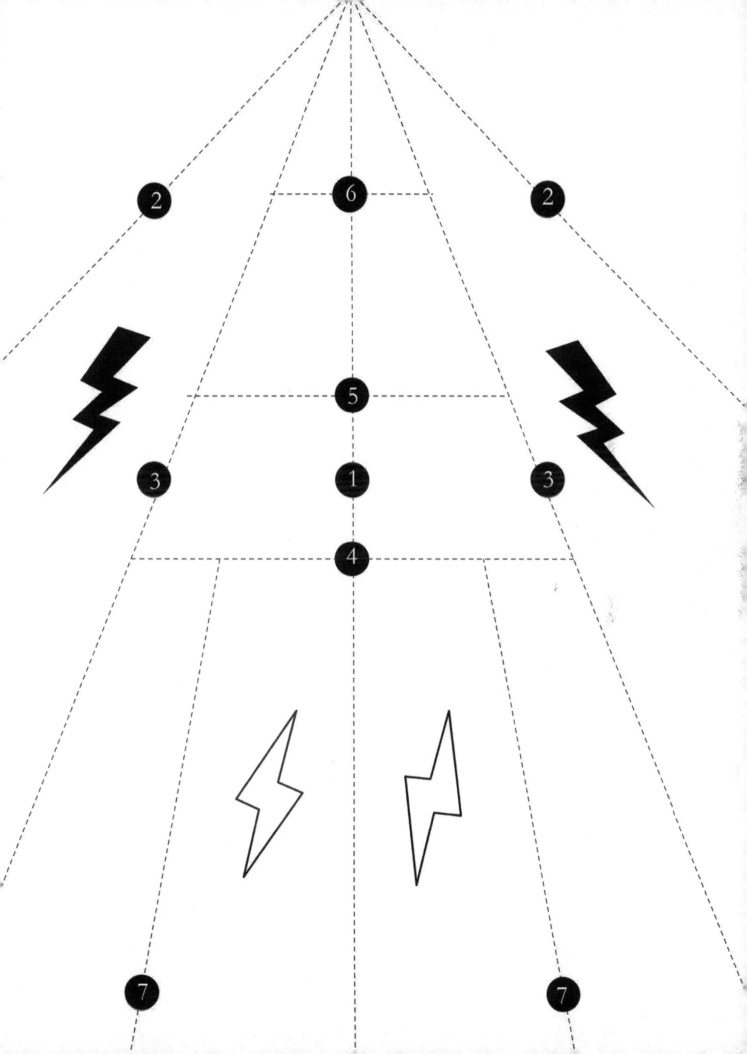

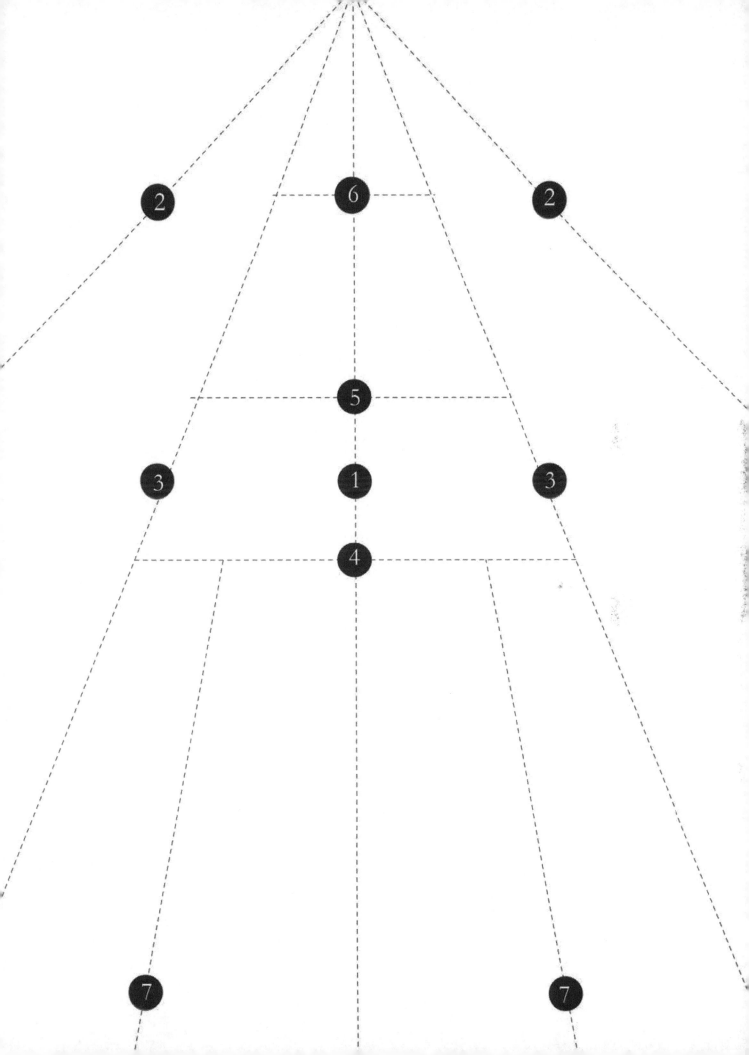

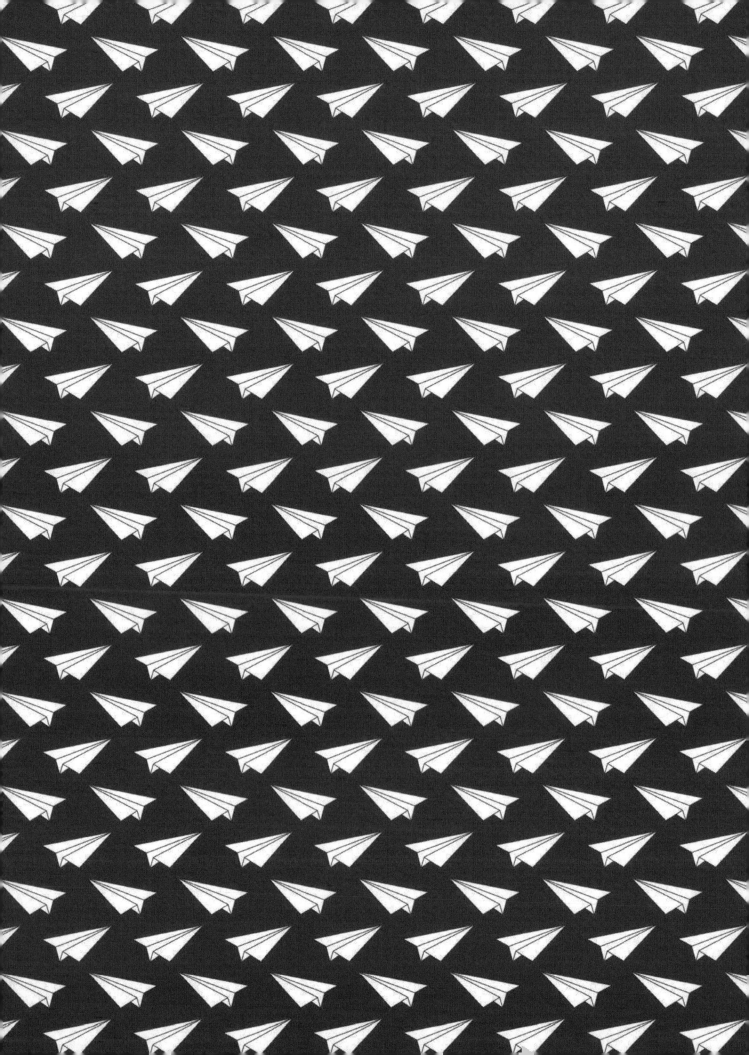

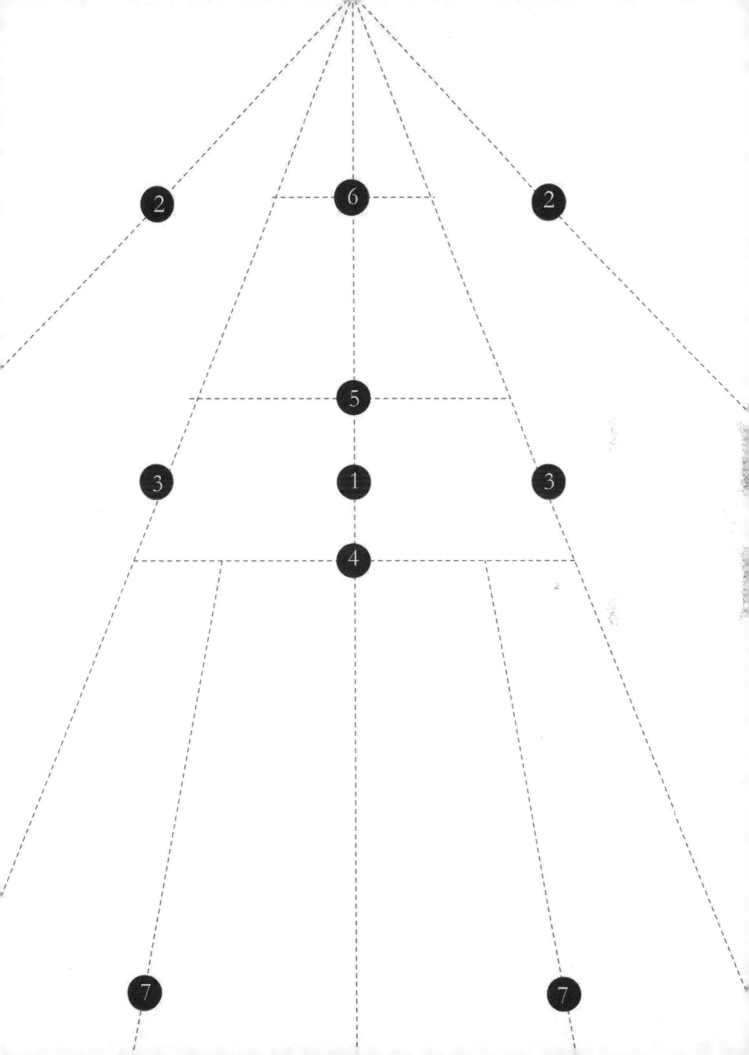

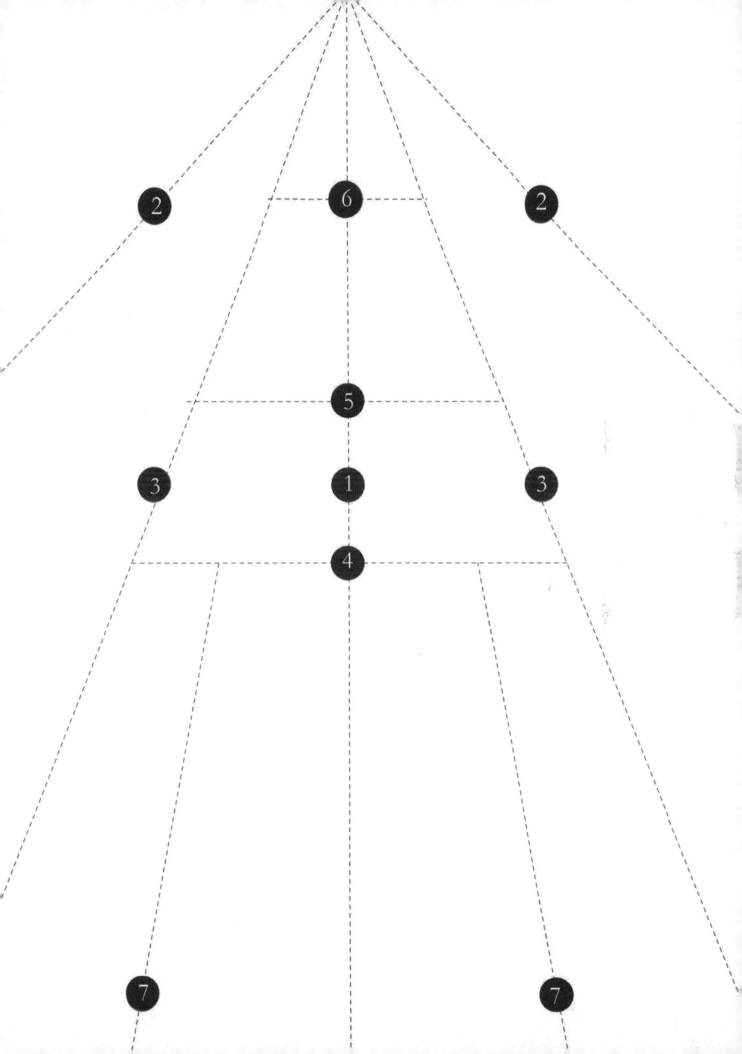

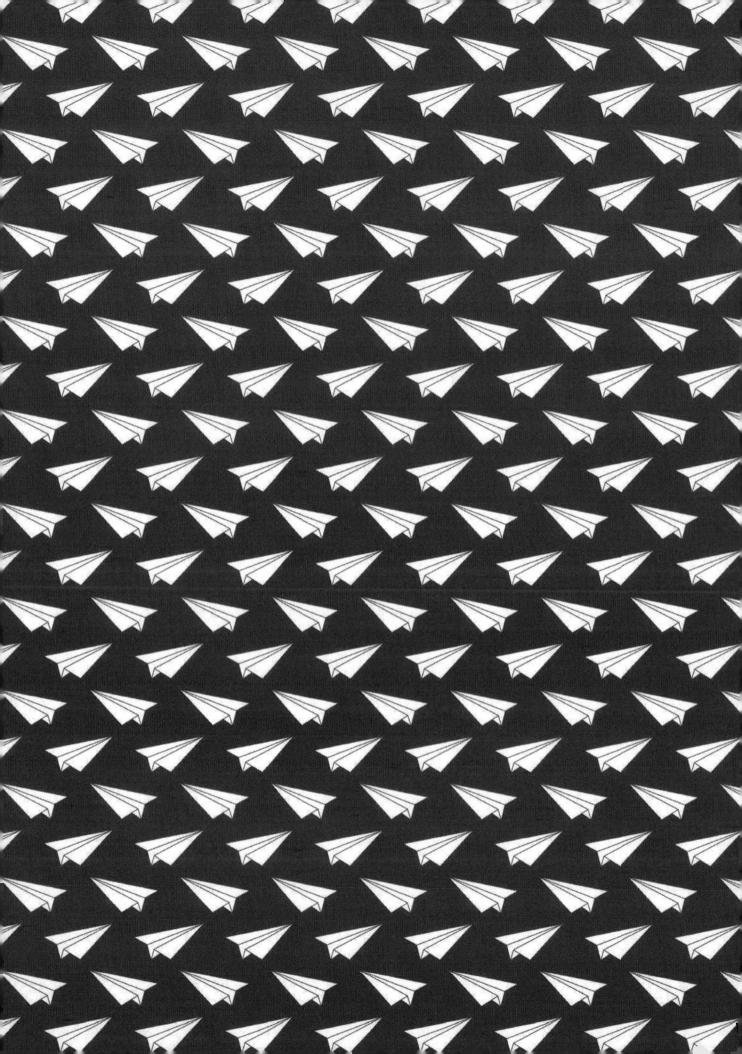

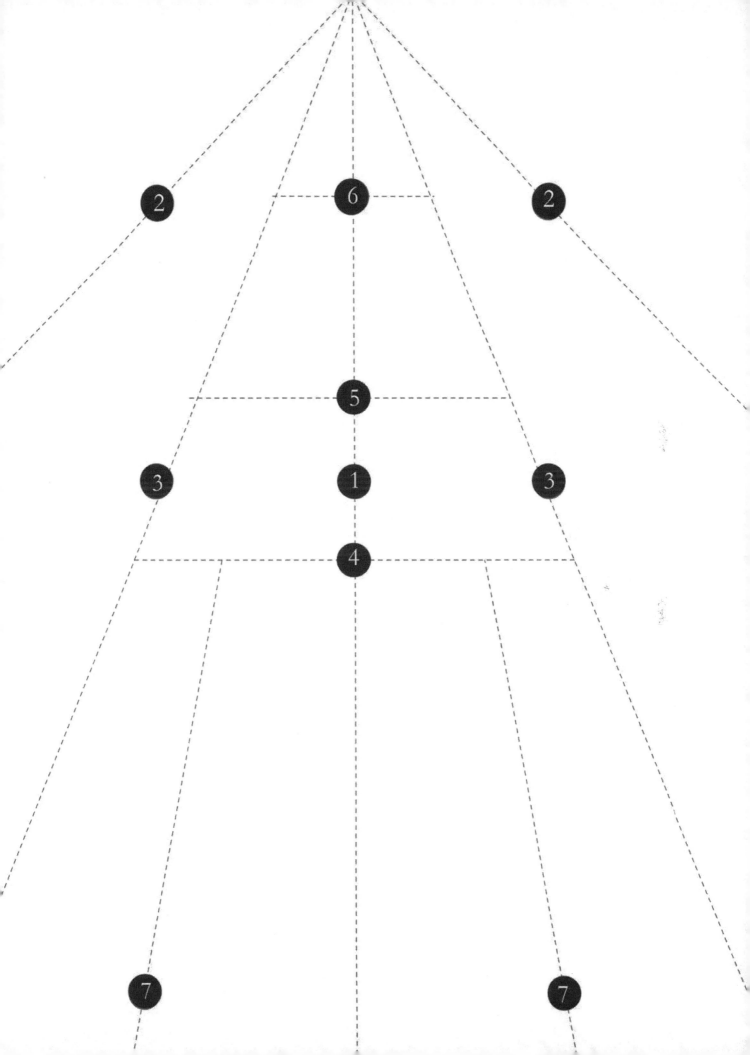

ORIGAMI PLANE - Cross Wing

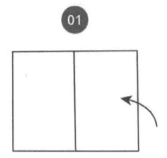

1. Fold the paper in half widthwise.

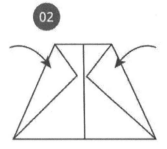

2. Fold the top corners to the center line so that the fold goes straight to the bottom corners.

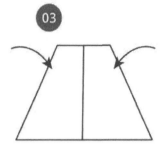

3. Now, open up the sheet and accordion fold the top corners in.

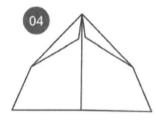

4. Fold the top corners to the center line.

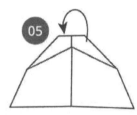

5. Fold the tip back about one inch.

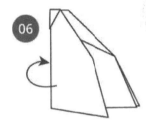

6. Fold the plane in half towards you.

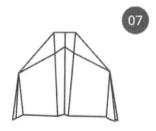

7. Fold out the sides to create the wings. Fold the wing tips up or down to create stabilizers.

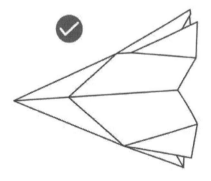

Final Paper Airplane Design
The wingtips in the final step can be folded either up or down depending on your preferences. Try both! Fold two of them up and two of them down for a dramatic look.

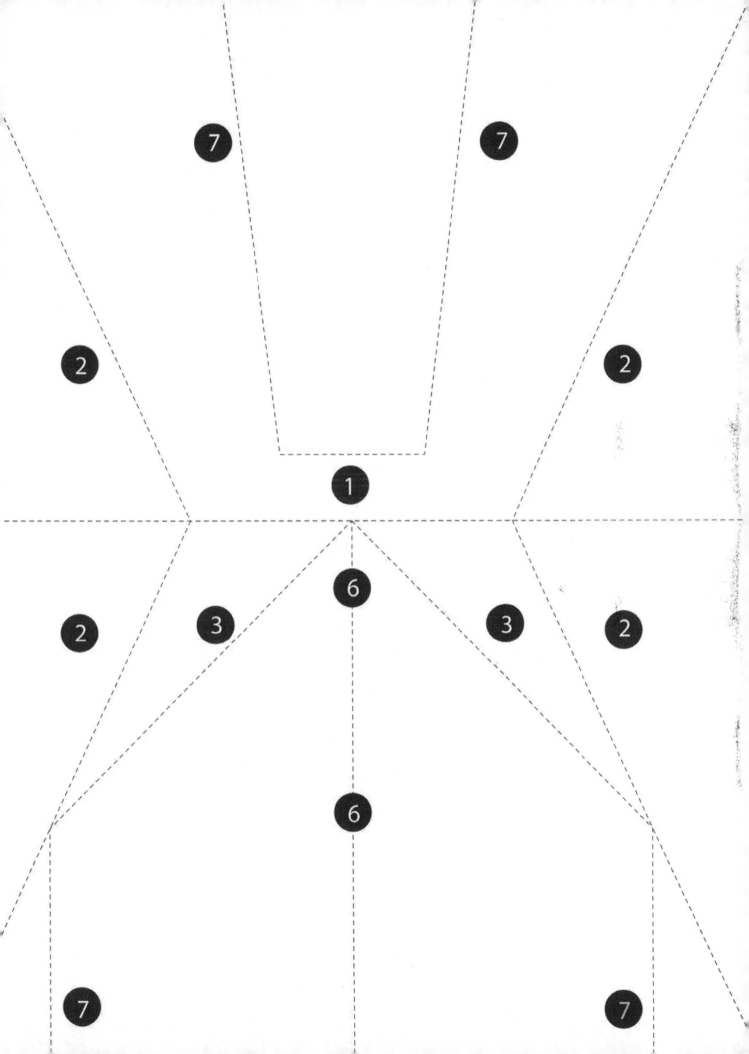

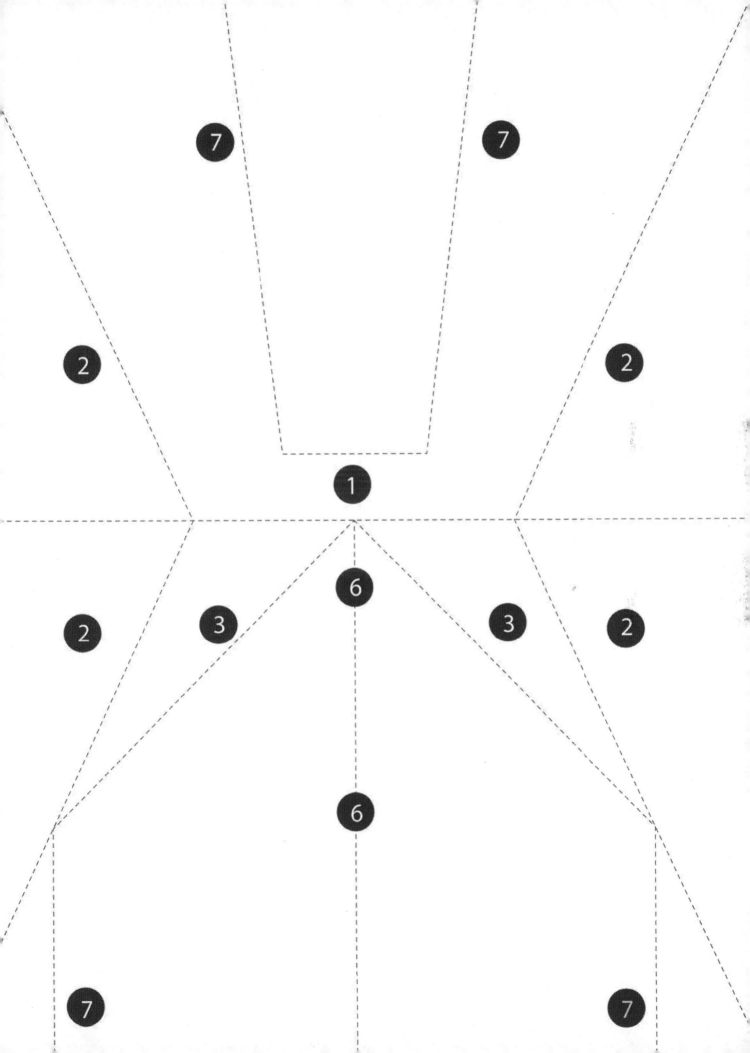

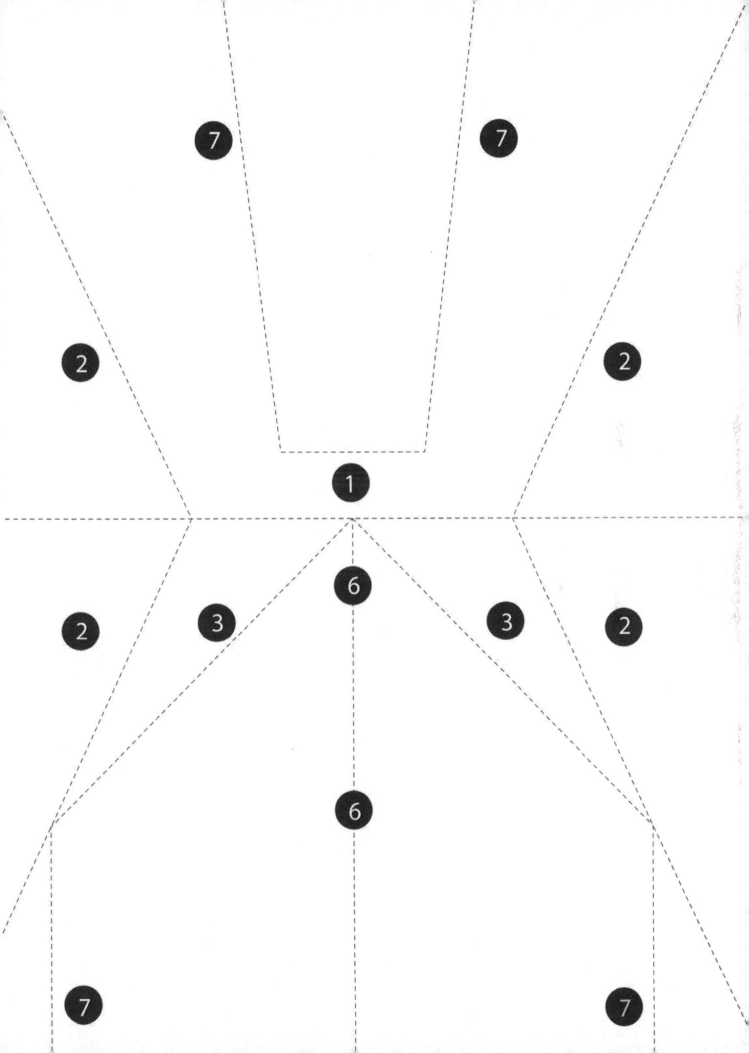

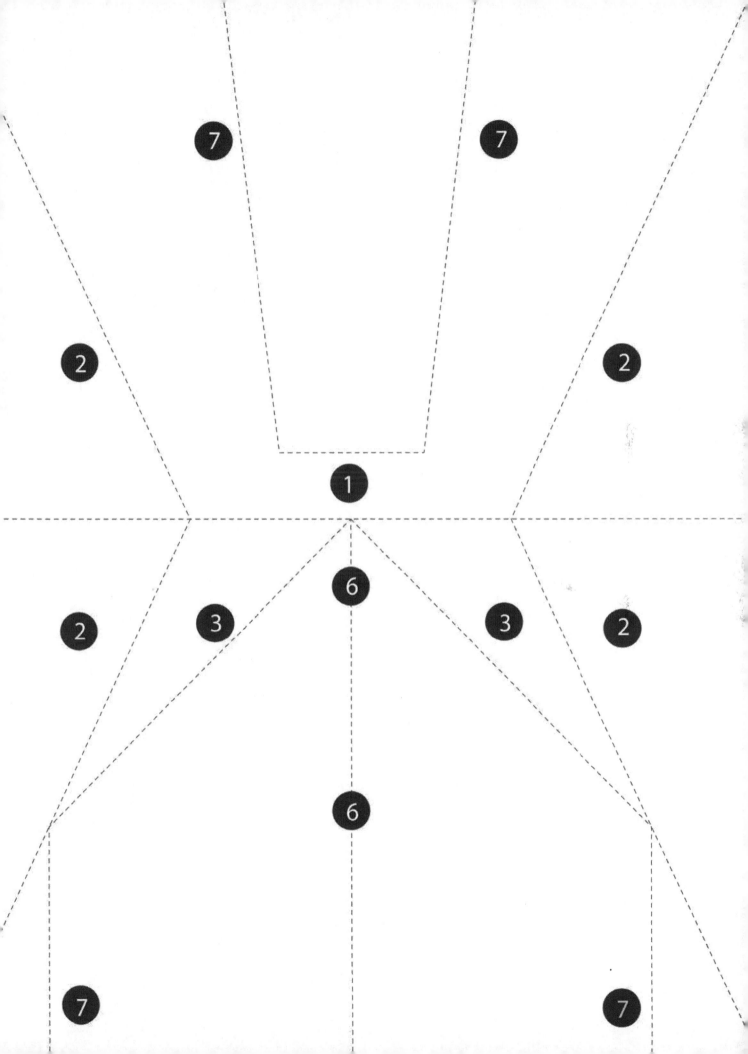

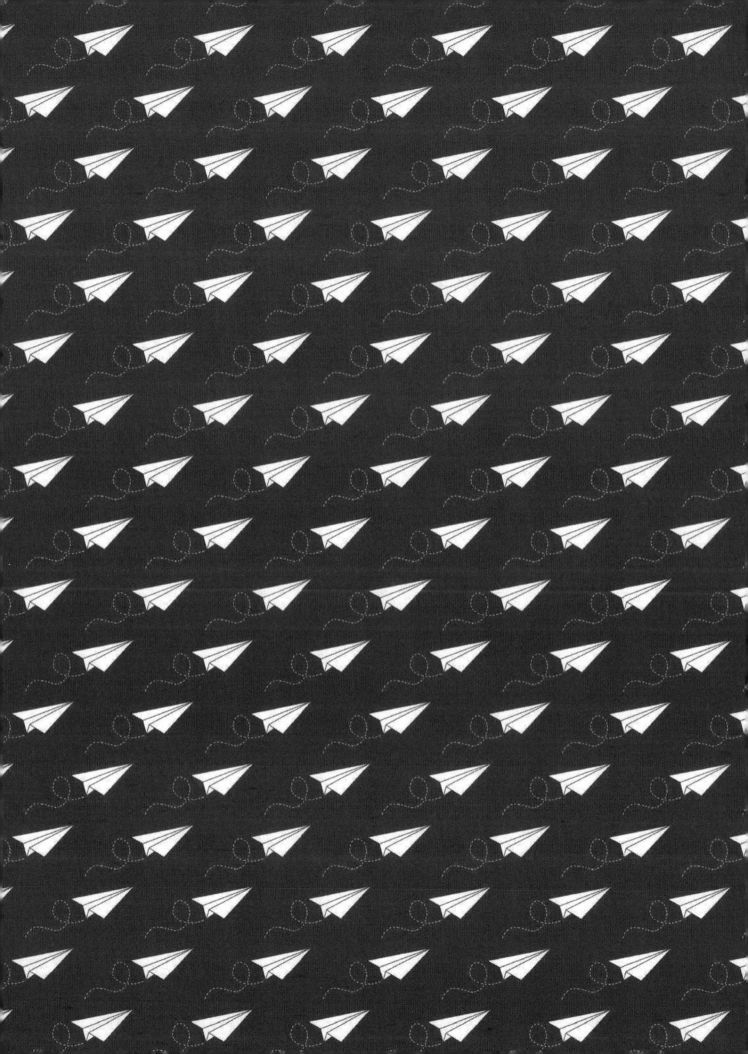

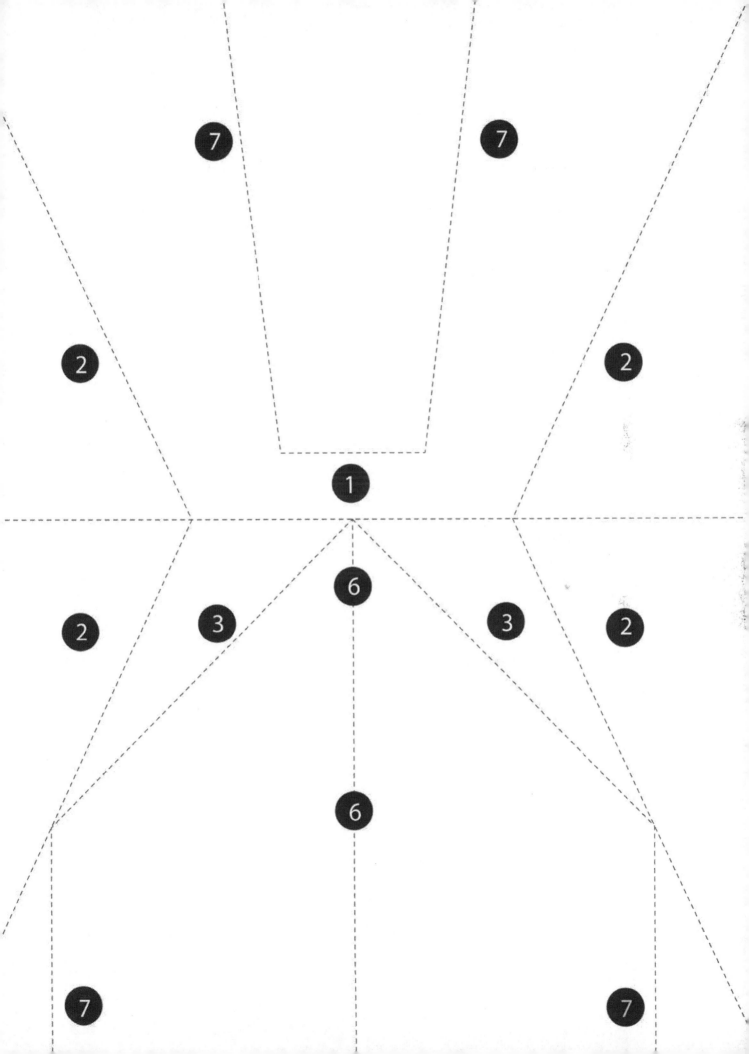

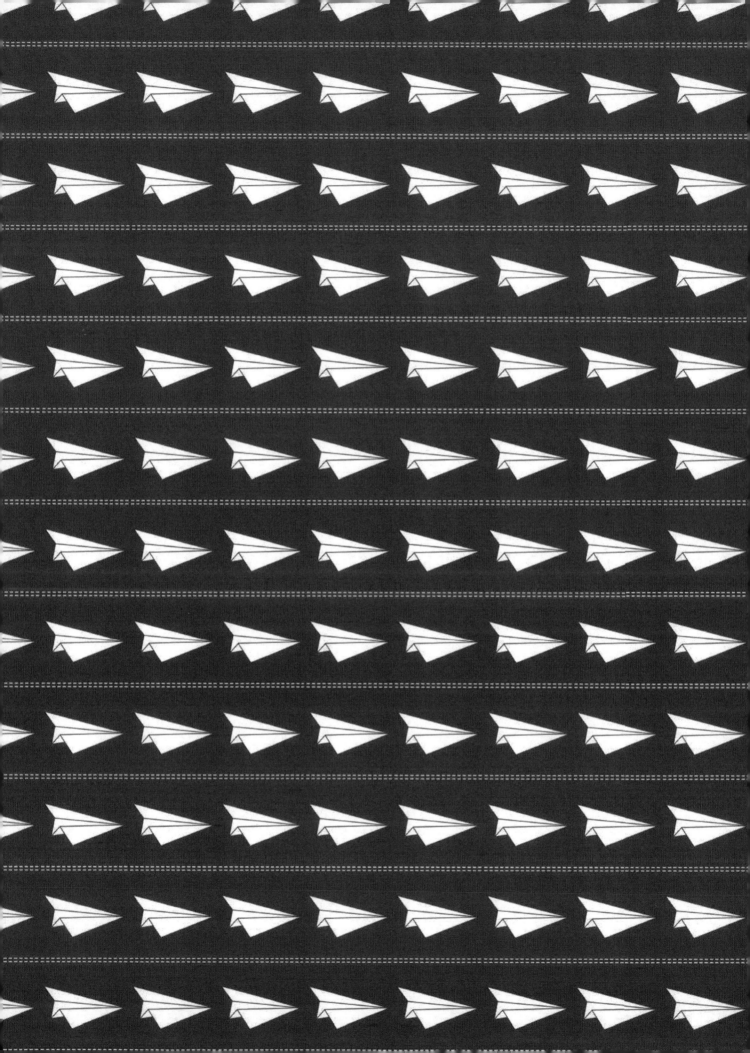

HARD FLYERS

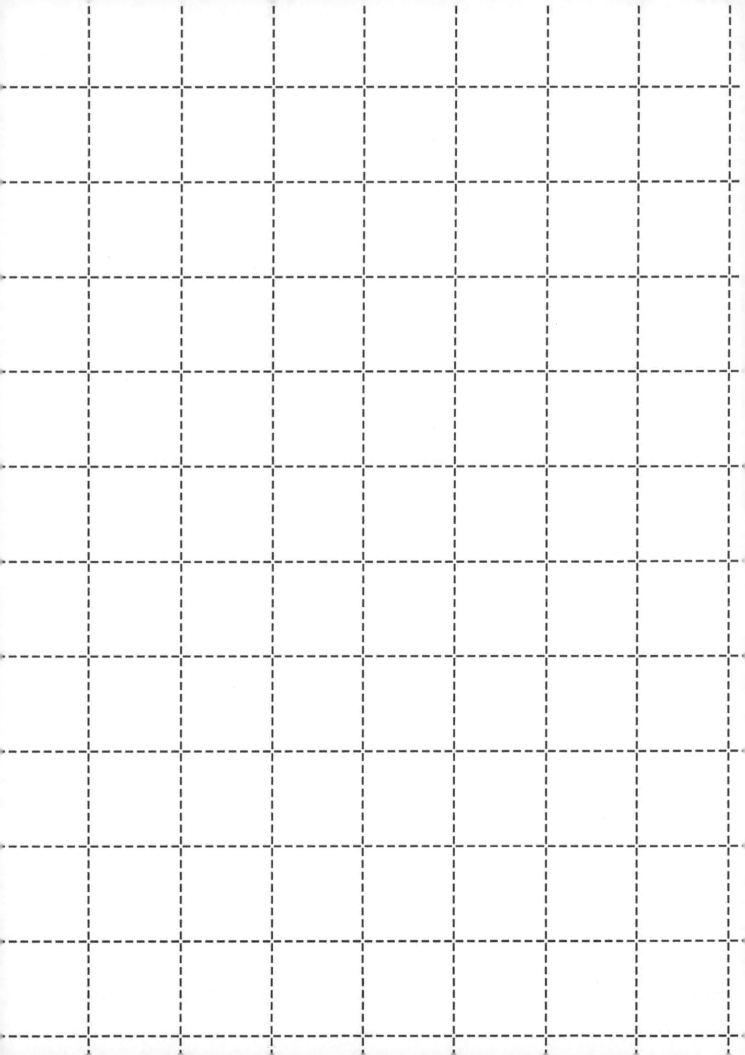

ORIGAMI PLANE - The BUZZER

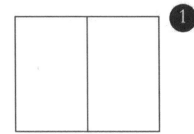

1. Fold the paper in half.

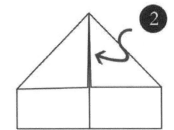

2. Unfold and then fold the top corners to the center line.

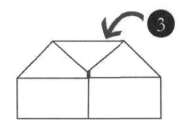

3. Fold the top peak down to the edge of the previous fold.

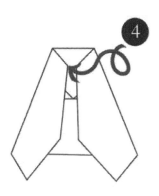

4. Fold the upper sides to the center line.

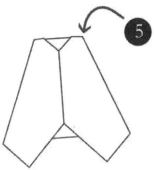

5. Fold the top about 1/2 inch away from you.

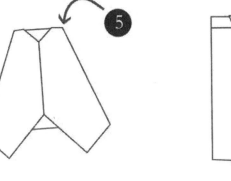

6. Fold the plane in half towards you.

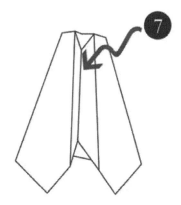

7. Fold both flaps out to create the wings. The body will be about a half inch tall. You may want a small piece of tape on the top to keep the wings from popping up or separating

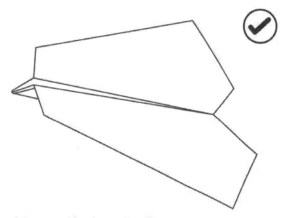

Final Paper Airplane Design
Use a bit of tape to keep this design from popping open in mid-flight. You can make small bends to the large triangular ailerons at the rear of the airplane to adjust it for level flight. Experiment with throwing hard and gently to see what works best for you.

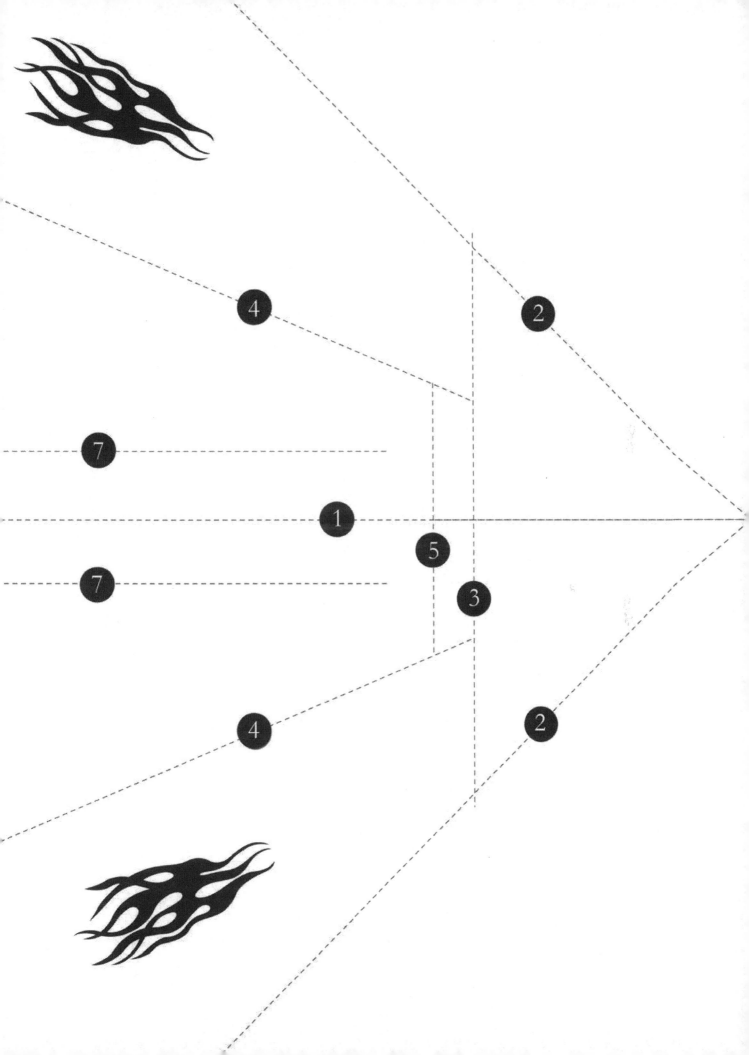

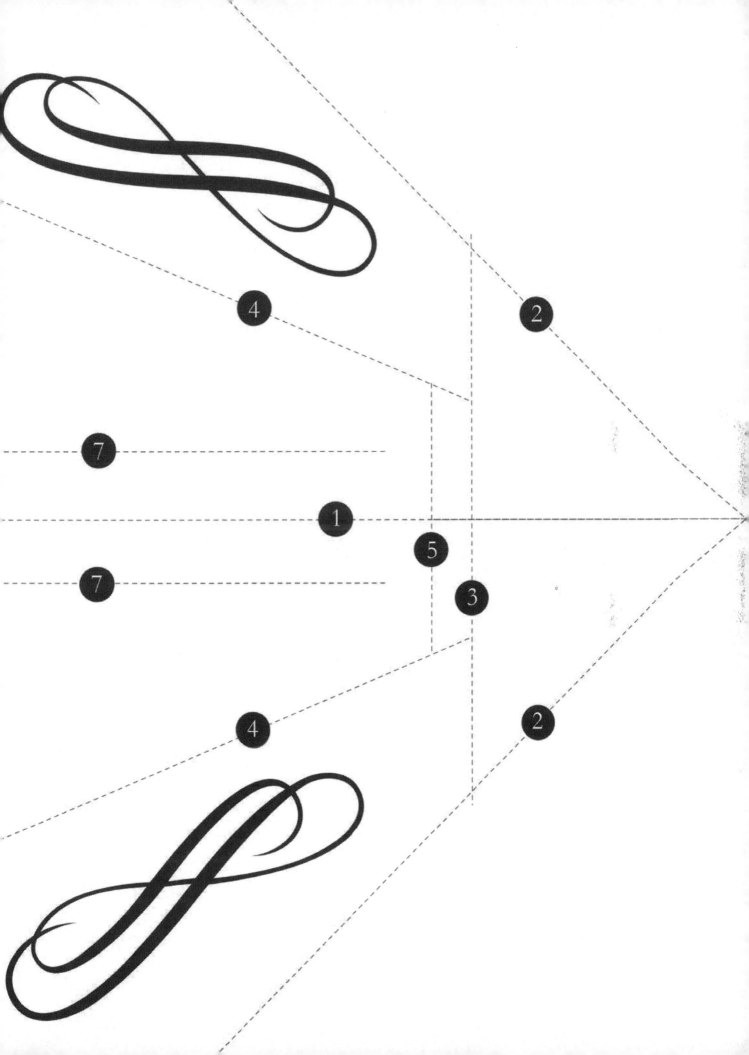

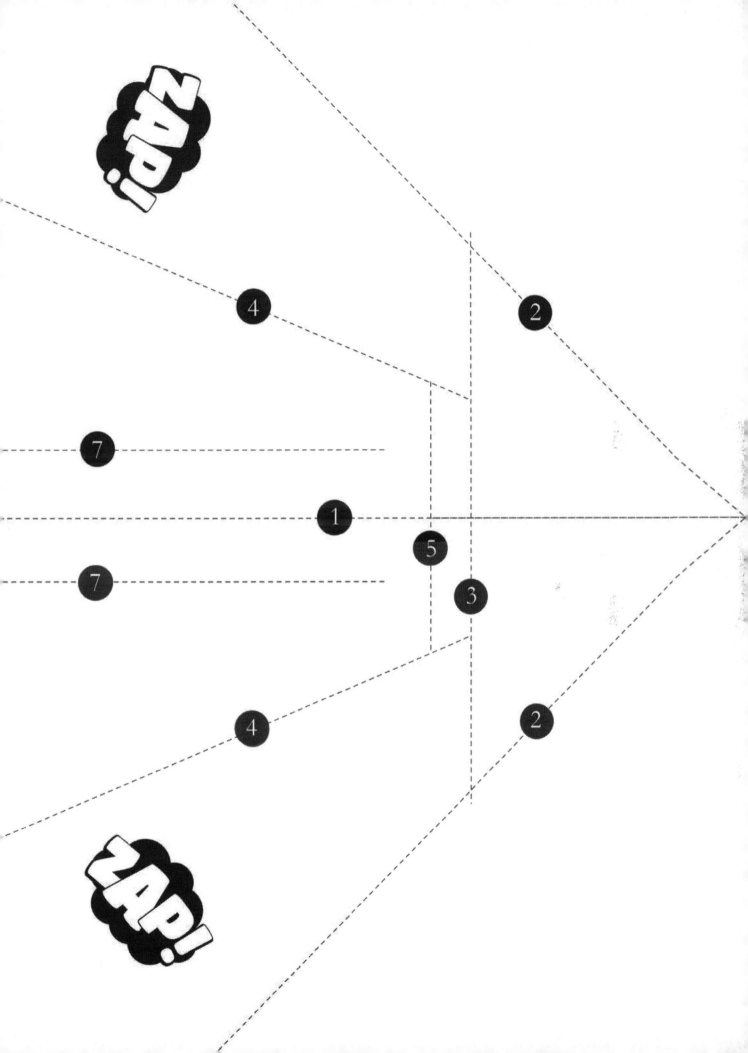

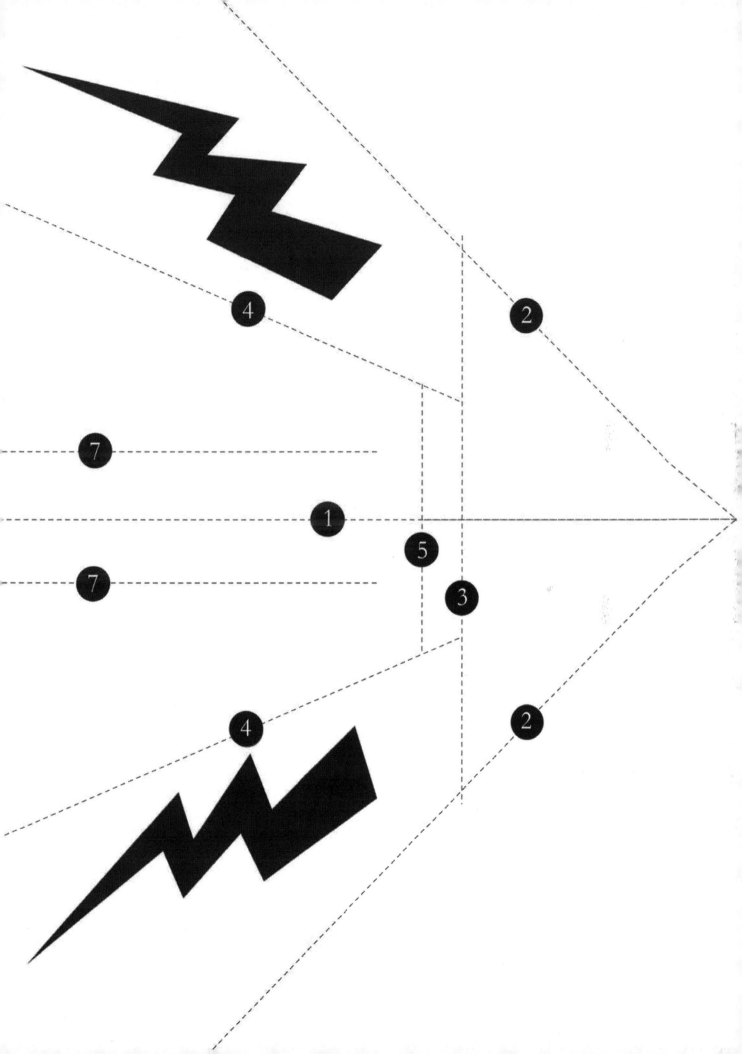

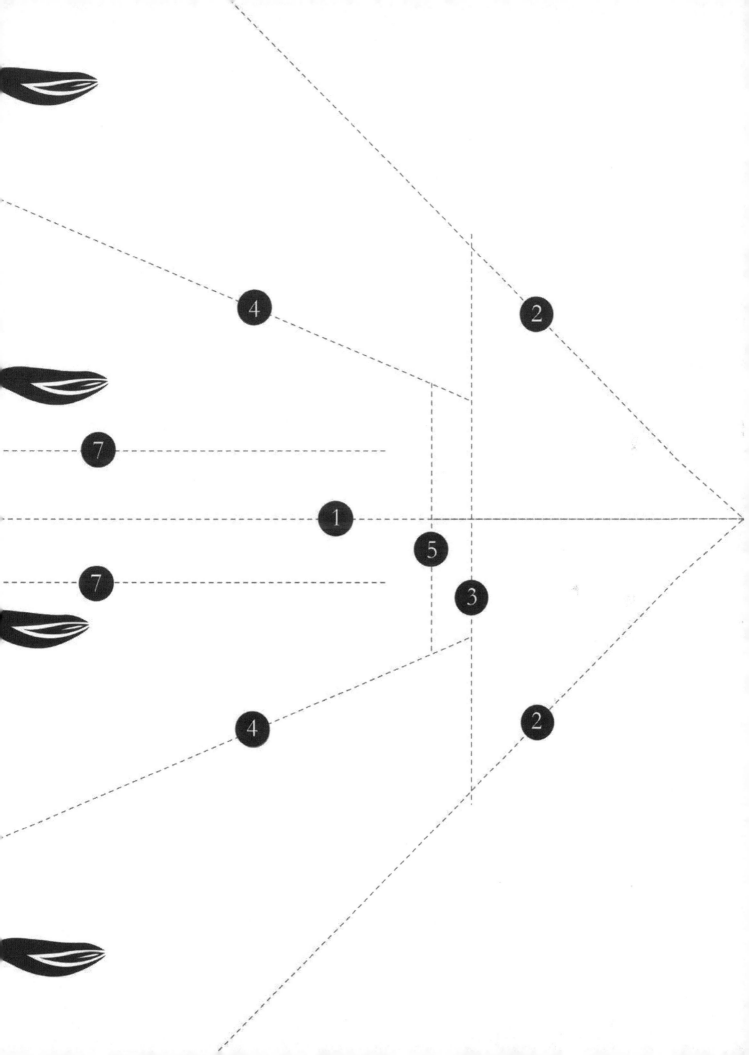

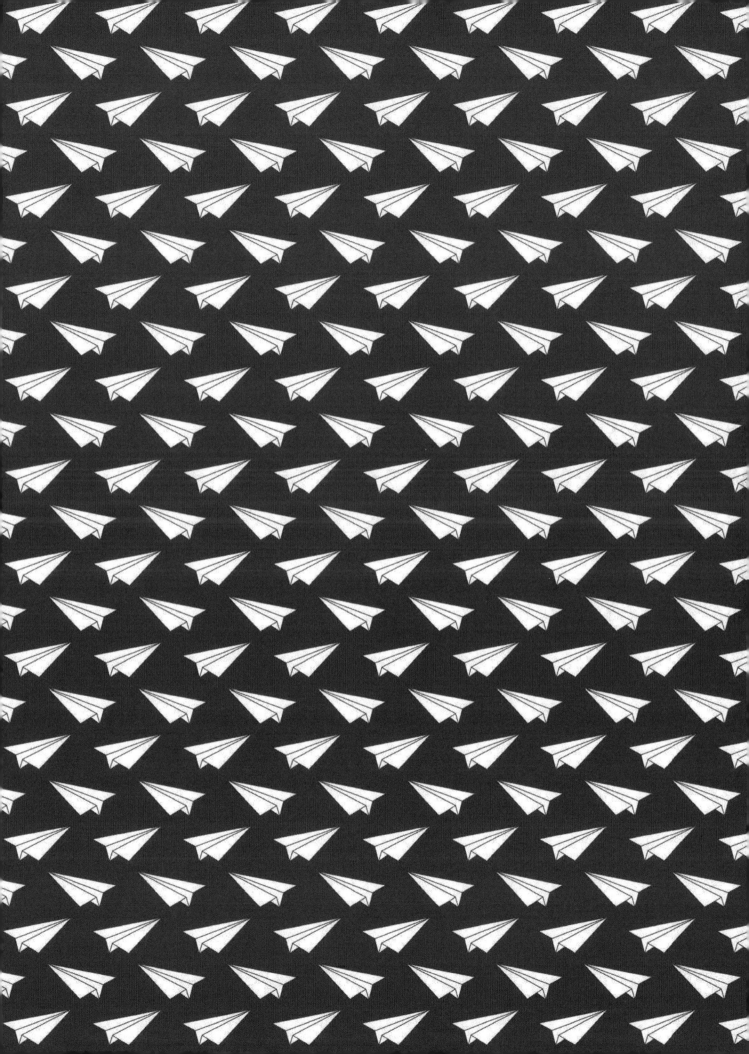

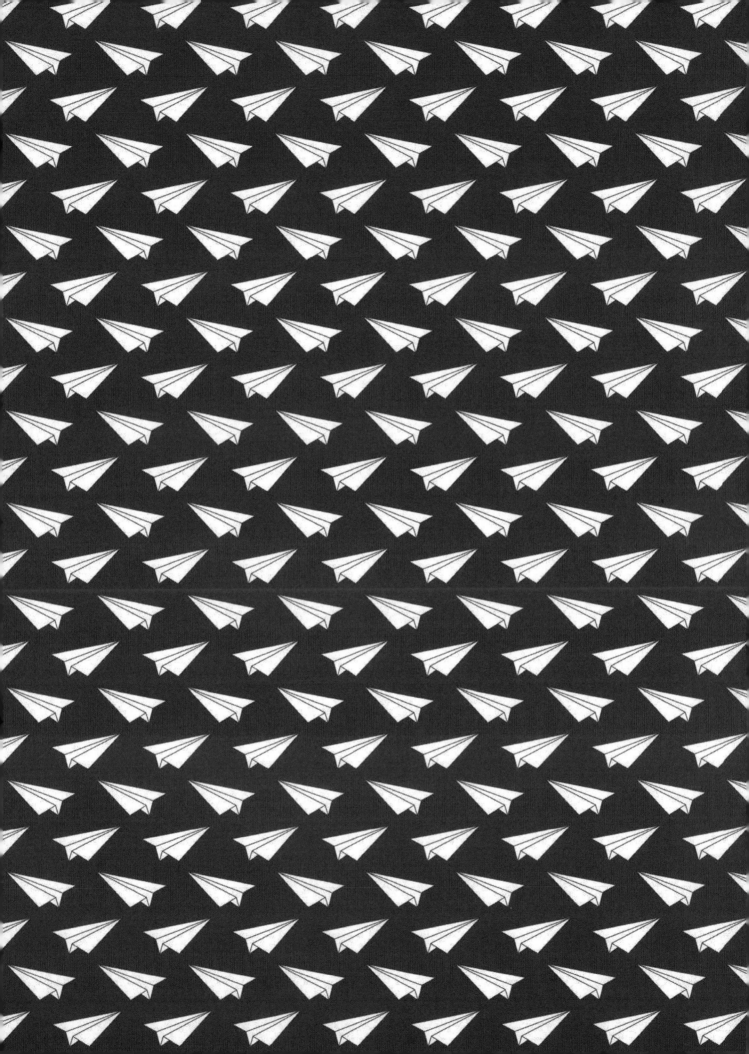

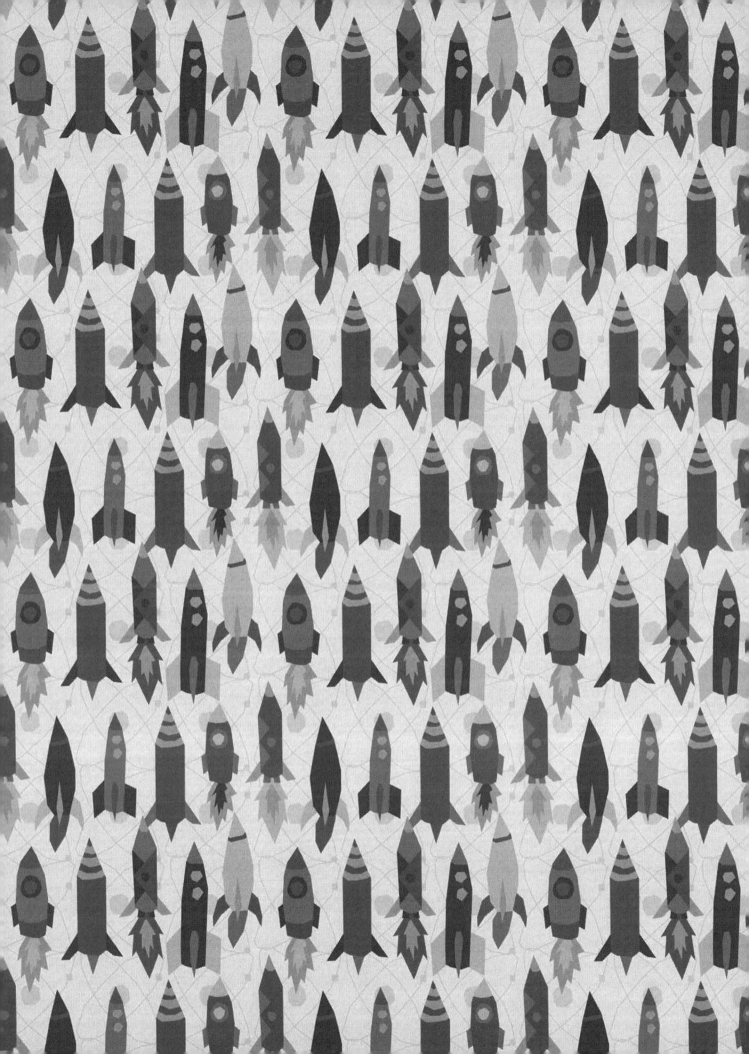

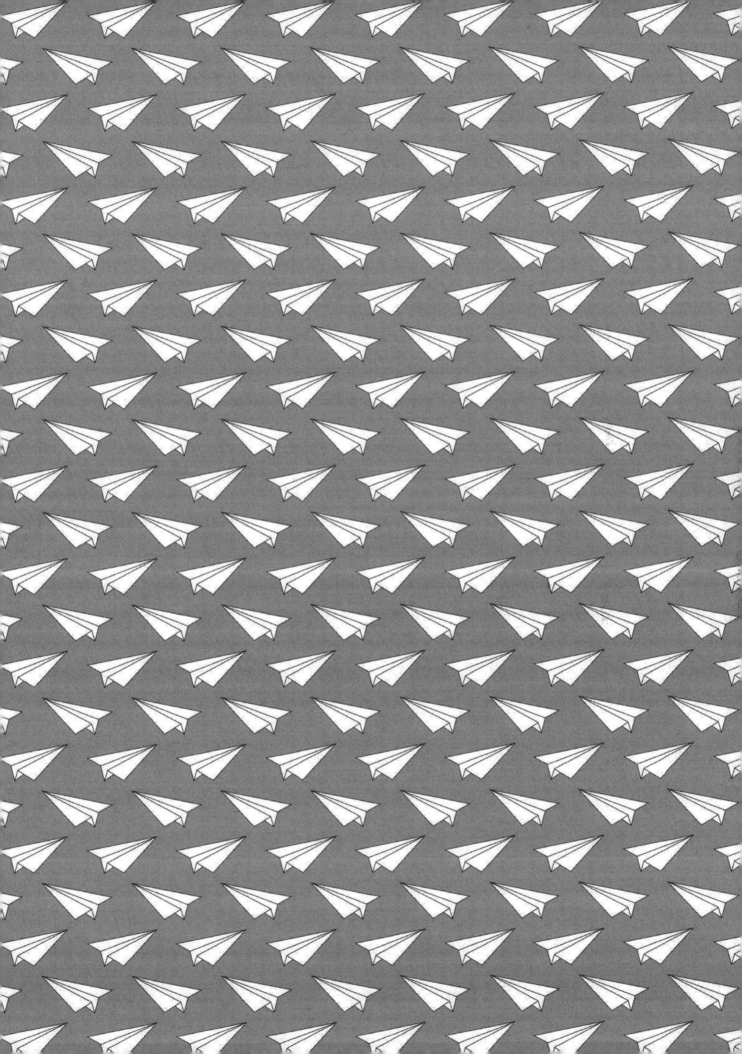

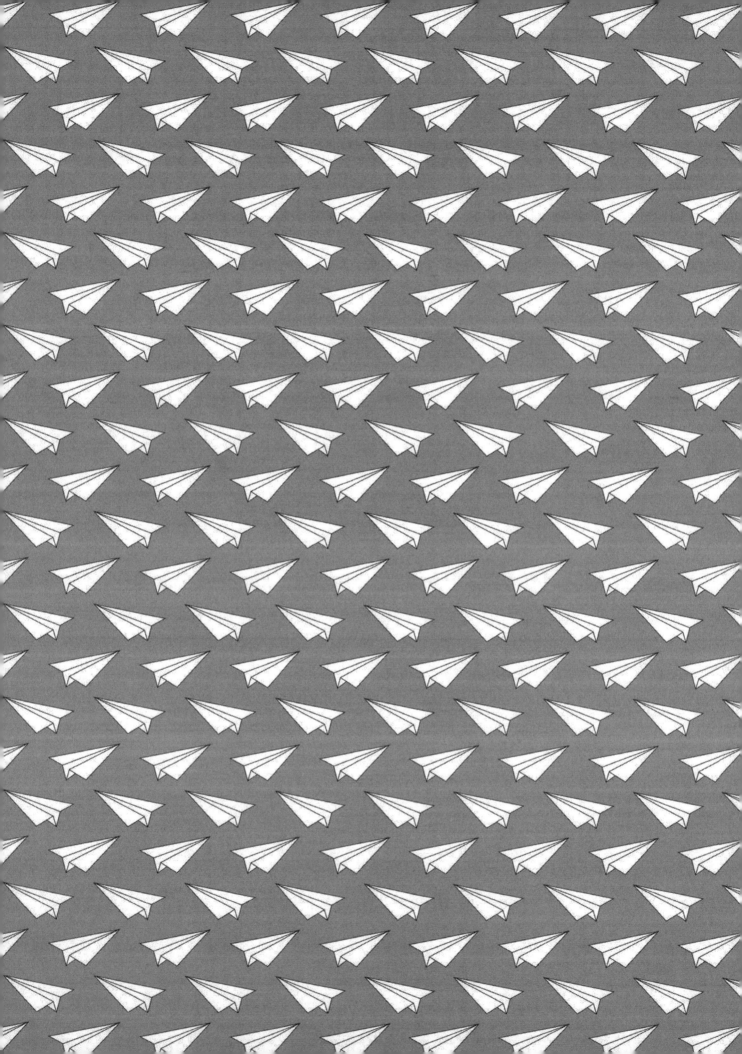

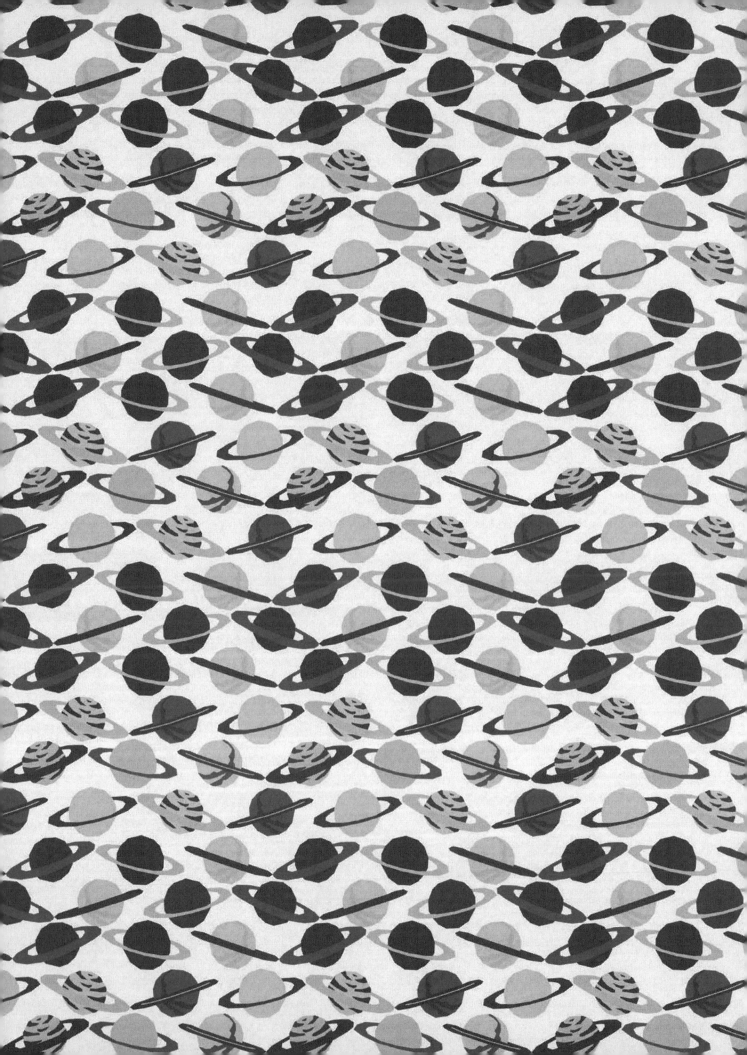

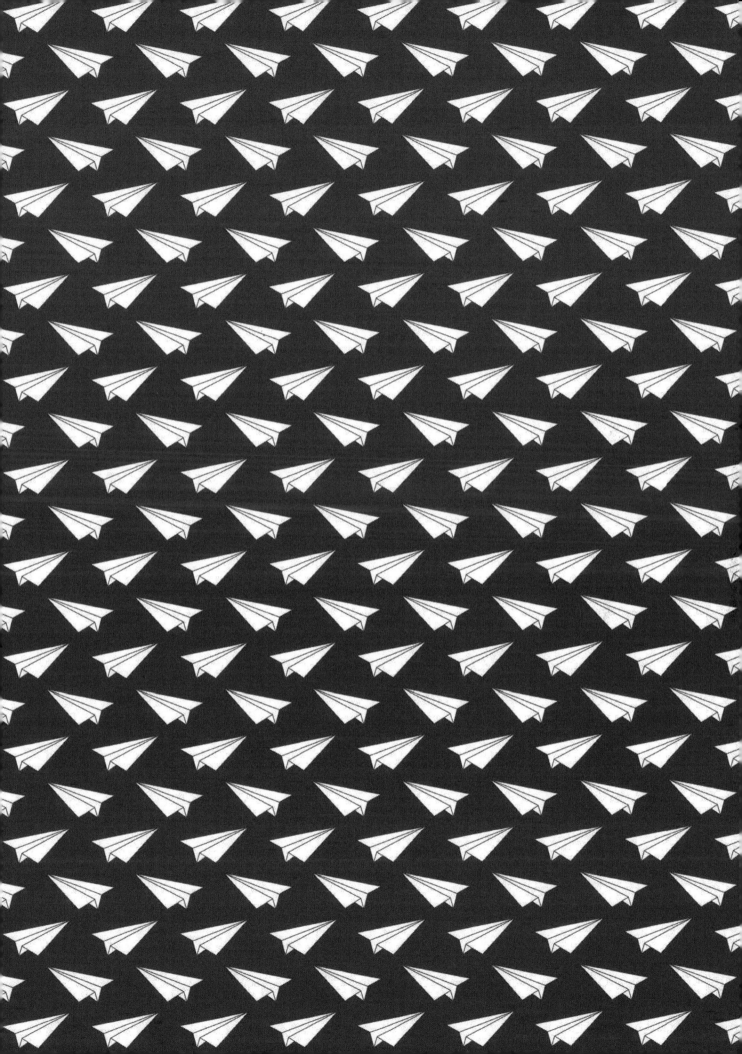

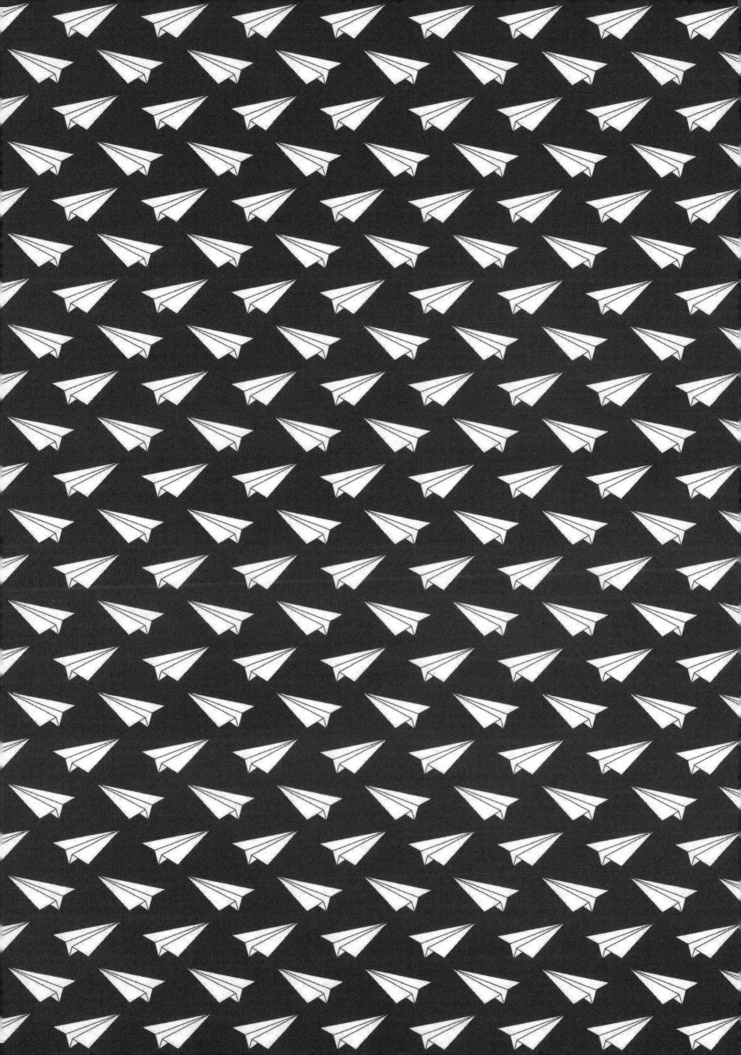

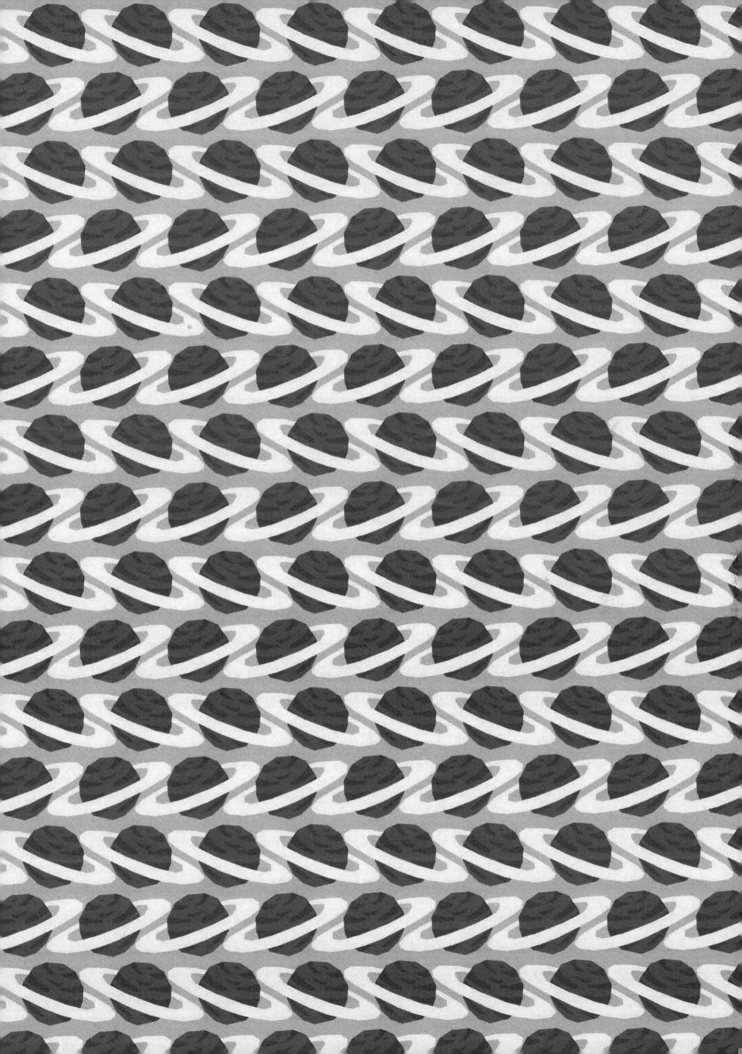

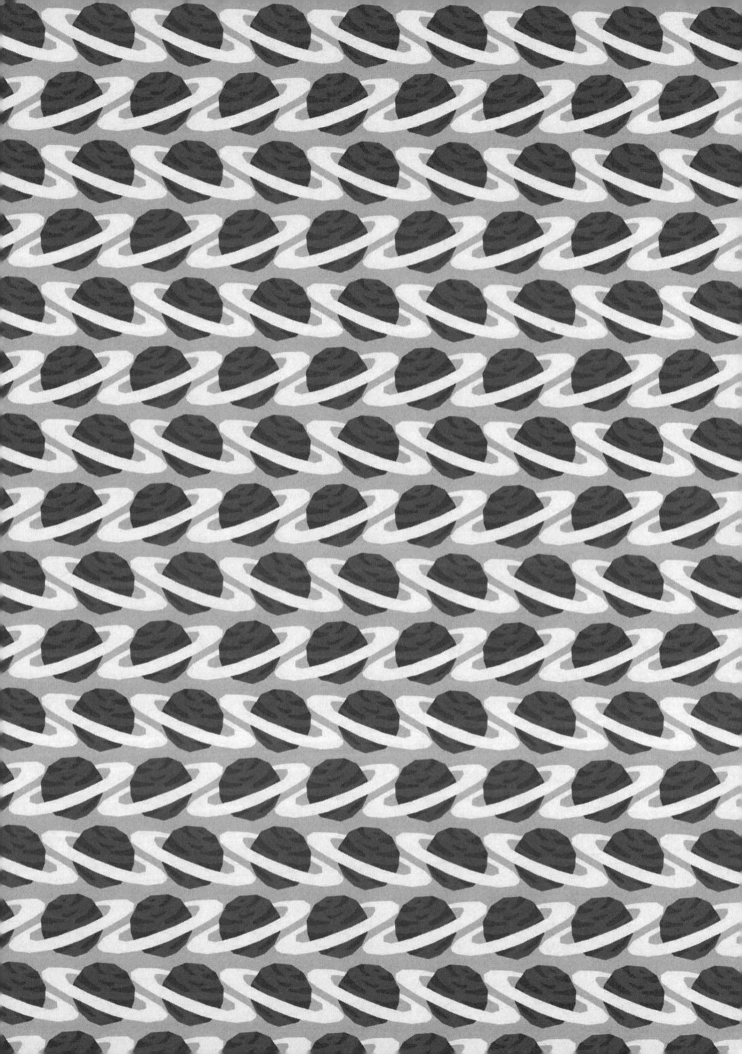

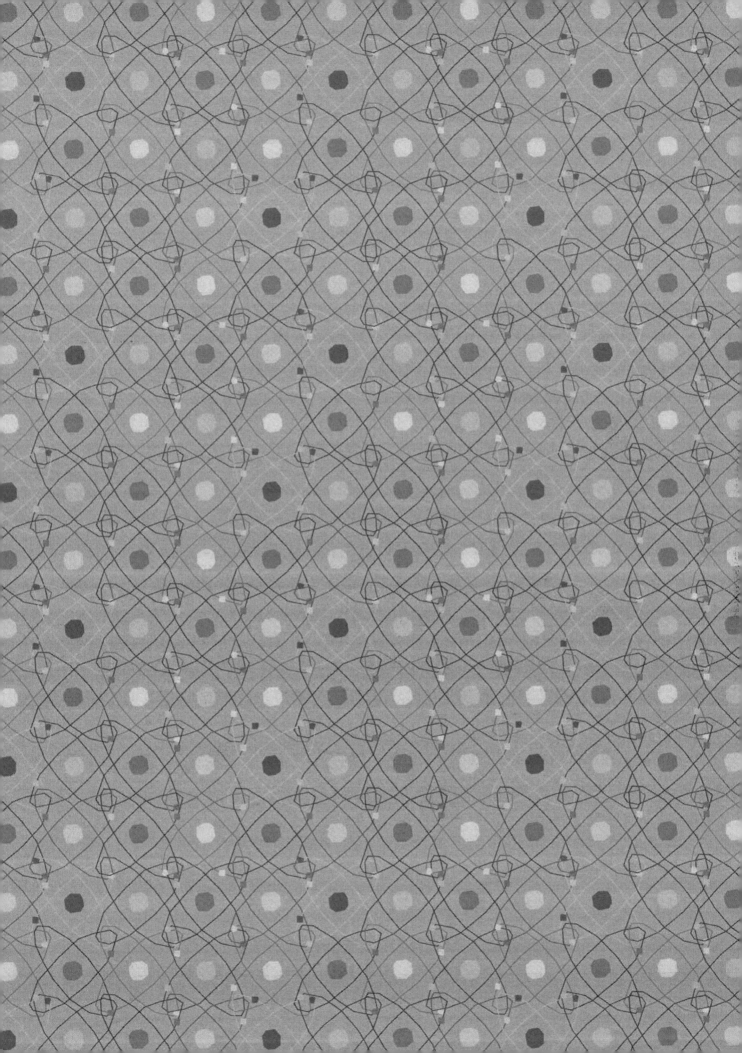

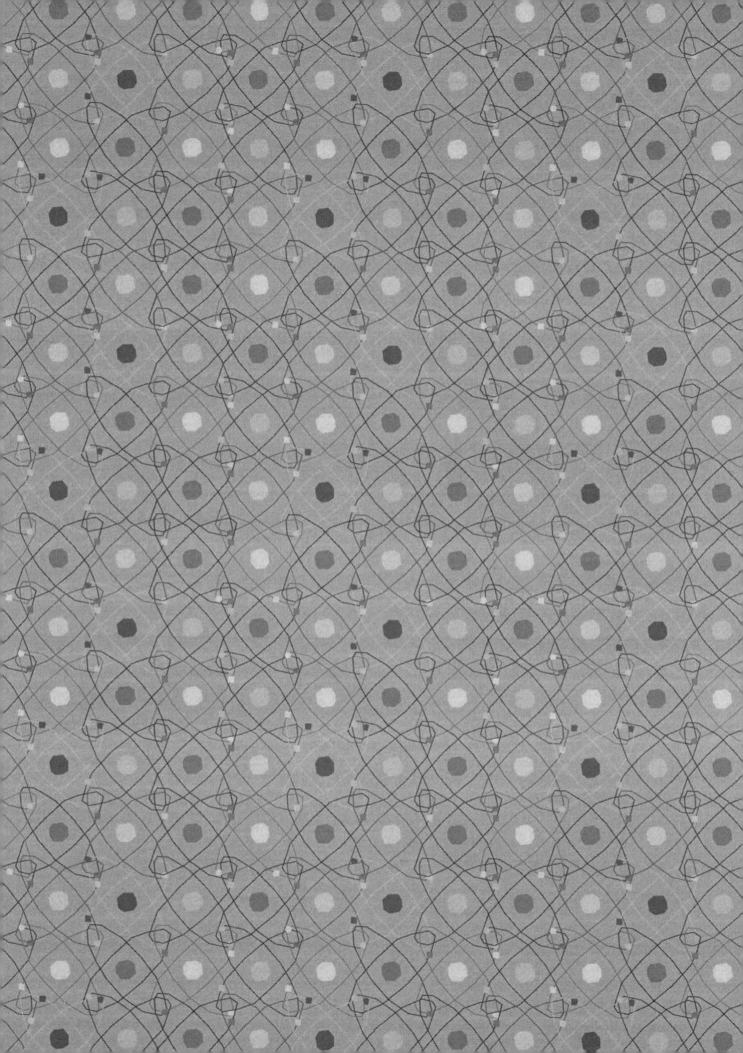

ENJOY THE BOOK?
CHECK OUT THESE TITLES

GREAT BOOKS AT GREAT PRICES

BY BUYING THIS BOOK YOU ARE SUPPORTING OUR LITTLE FAMILY AND SMALL BUSINESS GROW.

IF YOU ARE NOT INTRESTED IN THE OTHER TITLES, WE ASK YOU LEAVE US A REVIEW ON AMAZON BECAUSE IT HELPS MORE THAN KNOW!

THANK YOU,

MAX WATERS

Printed in Great Britain
by Amazon

28792764R00066